Research Methodology

An Introduction

Second Edition

Wayne Goddard and Stuart Melville

Research Methodology: An Introduction

First published in 1996
Second edition 2001
Reprinted 2005
Reprinted November 2006
Reprinted February 2007

P.O. Box 24309, Lansdowne 7779

ISBN 9780702156601

Copy editing: FPP Productions
Proofing: Cecily van Gend
Indexing: Cecily van Gend
Cover design: The Pumphaus Design Studio
Typesetting by Mckore Graphics, Panorama
Printing and binding: Mega Digital

Contents

Preface

In this book we have attempted to provide a comprehensive guide to research and how it is conducted. If research is seen as a continual journey then the aim of this text is to provide a road-map for the beginner.

The book covers every facet of the research process: finding and defining a suitable problem, performing literature surveys, conducting the research, analysing the results, and reporting the findings.

This text is intended for the beginning postgraduate or advanced undergraduate student, and no prior knowledge of research is assumed. It includes specific coverage of the techniques and methods of research used in science, engineering and technology, as well as those used in the human sciences. The book is designed for a one-semester course, but has sufficient material for a year-long course if the lecturer opts for a detailed treatment of all chapters. It is also appropriate for new researchers needing a guide for self-study.

A particular feature of the book is its concentration on South Africa, in contrast to the normal European or North American focus. While the research process may be the same, the system of universities and technikons, the funding bodies, and the country's research needs are not. Examples and case studies used are country-specific in order to make the text relevant to the South African reader.

The book is divided into five parts, each of which is largely self-contained.

Part 1 is on how to get started. This includes beginning postgraduate study, obtaining funding, the research process, preparing a statement of the research problem, and obtaining information from the literature.

Part 2 deals with the design of research and the collection of data. This includes sampling, the experimental method, laboratory work, simulation, and collecting data from people.

Part 3 deals with the analysis of data. It explains how to organise, summarise and depict data, and provides a range of tools for statistical estimation and testing. No prior knowledge of statistics is assumed.

Part 4 deals with scientific writing, including questions of style and referencing, and describes formats for reports such as theses, dissertations, and funding proposals.

Part 5 deals with broader issues in research. In addition to dealing with issues such as research ethics and the development of research thought, it also contains a chapter devoted to South Africa's particular research needs.

Discussion questions and exercises are provided at the end of the chapter. Answers to selected exercises appear in an appendix.

The referencing system used in this text is the 'FTL' (first-three-letters) scheme, which is discussed in Chapter 12, Referencing, and in Appendix A, A.3 Effectively FTL; A Referencing Example.

Stuart Melville and Wayne Goddard
Durban, 1996

Preface to the Second Edition

In the five years since the first edition, much has changed and much hasn't changed.

The Internet has flourished, both as a communication medium and as the home of the World Wide Web. The pace and amount of research continues to grow at a bewildering rate. Every day it becomes more important to be able to distil the real information from the mountains of data that we are bombarded with, and which the Internet provides.

At the same time, the fundamental methods of research have not changed.

The text has been revised to reflect these trends: the growing importance of the Internet, of other styles of research, and of issues in research. On the other hand, the coverage of statistics has been slightly reduced.

Nevertheless, the edition maintains a more scientific emphasis than most books on research methodology. And, more importantly, I have attempted to keep to the original goal of a to-the-point introduction to research and its methods.

Sadly, one of the authors, Stuart Melville, passed away in 1997. The second edition is dedicated to our new collaboration, Robert and Kate.

The material was successfully course-tested in 1995. We welcome comments, suggestions or queries, which should be addressed to:

goddard@nu.ac.za
Department of Computer Science
Desmond Clarence Building
University of Natal, Durban
Durban 4041

Wayne Goddard
Durban, June 2001

Acknowledgements

This book is the product of the co-operative efforts of a large number of people, and our grateful thanks go to all of them. The following people in particular deserve special mention:

- Celia Melville for her hard work in writing the chapter on the history and philosophy of research, and even harder work in keeping the chapter to a manageable size;
- Dr VL (Lingam) Pillay for information regarding Case Study 1;
- Dr Anwar Hoosen for information regarding Case Study 3;
- Prof. Leon Troskie for statistical advice;
- Thiruthlall (Nips) Nepal, Robyn Laing and Dr David Fraser for proof-reading the manuscript for the first edition;
- the Juta team (Gavin Stanford, Des Walker and John Linnegar for the first edition, and Solani Ngobeni and Sandie Vahl for the second edition);
- the ML Sultan B.Tech. (Information technology) class of 1995 for acting as our guinea-pigs.

Introduction

WHAT IS RESEARCH?

Research is not just a process of gathering information, as is sometimes suggested. Rather, it is about answering unanswered questions or creating that which does not currently exist. In many ways, research can be seen as a process of expanding the boundaries of our ignorance. The person who believes he/she knows everything reveals not only arrogance, but also a profound ignorance.

As people study the unknown (and as a result find new areas of ignorance), they often discover useful things. Everything we now know had to be discovered by someone at some time – without research you would be naked, homeless and penniless; and you would certainly not be reading this book!

The discovery and the creation of knowledge, therefore, lies at the heart of research, or as Leedy puts it, research is 'a systematic quest for undiscovered knowledge' (Lee89). Good research is 'systematic' in that it is planned, organised and has a specific goal.

It is also a never-ending process: discoveries and creations lead to new discoveries and new creations, and so on. As you read this, millions of people around the world are involved in research, some of it minor, some major. It is the ways in which people can go about research that this book discusses.

Two famous examples

In 1897, a young student named Marie Curie started work on her doctoral thesis. The previous year, the physicist Antoine Becquerel had detected radiation emanating from uranium, and Curie set out to study the phenomenon of radioactivity. After examining several uranium compounds, she concluded that the amount of radiation produced was proportional to the amount of uranium involved. However, uranium pitchblende (the principal source of uranium) was an exception to this rule, for it produced four times more radiation than could be expected from the uranium content.

In trying to explain this phenomenon, Curie theorised that there must be some other, hitherto undiscovered, element causing the high levels of radiation. Her husband, Pierre, joined her in her research, and from tons of pitchblende they eventually isolated tiny quantities of two previously undiscovered elements, polonium and radium. In 1903 Marie Curie obtained her doctorate and also won the Nobel prize for physics (shared with Pierre Curie and Becquerel) for this work. (In 1911 she received another Nobel prize, this time for chemistry.)

The research of Marie and Pierre Curie was the basis of further research on the atom, which led ultimately to the splitting of the atom in 1938. This in turn prompted the Manhattan Project – the research programme aimed at building an atomic bomb.

Two designs were pursued for the bomb: one using the uranium isotope U_{235} and the other using the radioactive element plutonium. Enrico Fermi used plutonium in 1942 in the first nuclear reactor, which was built in a basement at the University of Chicago. At the weapons laboratory at Los Alamos, in New Mexico, a team under the physicist J. Robert Oppenheimer surrounded the plutonium with explosives designed to compress it into a mass capable of sustained chain reaction. At Alamogordo, on July 16, 1945, the first atomic bomb was detonated. A few weeks later, atomic bombs were dropped on Hiroshima and Nagasaki (Gro95).

These two examples demonstrate many of the fundamental features of research. Curie was a postgraduate student who had to work largely on her own with extremely limited funds on a project designed to acquire knowledge for its own sake. (No one at that stage knew the effects of radioactive material.) The Manhattan Project, on the other hand, was a huge project involving the United States Army, government departments and a number of universities, with an unprecedented funding budget and access to hundreds of the best minds of the time from several countries, all harnessed to solving a specific problem. Despite their different natures, both projects entailed observing, theorising, experimenting to test the theories, drawing conclusions and reporting the results; in other words, they both used the **scientific method.**

The results of these projects also opened up new questions and sparked further research. Curie's work, for example, started a chain of research that led not just to the atomic bomb and nuclear power, but to the whole field of nuclear physics, where today thousands of questions are being asked – and then answered using the scientific method.

WHY DO RESEARCH?

Asking why people do research is in many cases the same as asking why people ask 'why?' about the universe in which they live. The pursuit of knowledge purely in order to know *why* is as old as humankind, and much research is the result of this pursuit. Research can also result from specific real-world *needs* – the need for low-cost housing, for example, or a more powerful radio transmitter, or even an atomic bomb. A third, often overlooked, impetus to do research is the pursuit of postgraduate qualifications: would the study of nuclear physics be as advanced today if Marie Curie had decided against doing her doctorate?

Research is sometimes labelled as either **pure** or **applied** research. Pure research is held to be research performed for the single goal of gaining knowledge, or, to put it another way, of gaining 'knowledge for knowledge's sake'. Any practically useful outcomes of the research are simply a bonus. The alternative is applied research, which is performed to solve a specific practical problem. Here the practically useful outcome is the goal of the research, and any outcomes of theoretical significance are the bonus.

Such a division seems naturally appealing to the type of person who likes to divide things into two classes. (As opposed to the other type, who doesn't!) Certainly, Curie's work seems very much pure research in pursuit of knowledge, while the atom bomb project seems very much applied research to fill a specific need. However, Curie's pure research led to the applied research on the bomb, and this applied research generated many new theoretical questions. The overlap between pure and applied research is, in fact, so pronounced that all research today has both pure and applied elements to it.

WHERE DOES RESEARCH OCCUR?

In South Africa, research is carried out at museums, universities, technikons, industry research laboratories, councils such as the Council for Scientific and Industrial Research (CSIR), the Human Sciences Research Council (HSRC) and the Medical Research Council (MRC), and various state departments. For the staff in such institutions, research is not just postgraduate study, it is a career.

The name of the Human Sciences Research Council embodies the fact that *all research is scientific*, and all researchers are scientists, regardless of their field of work. The research economist or social scientist is just as much a scientist as the research chemist or computer scientist.

WHAT DO RESEARCHERS USE?

Leedy (Lee89) includes the following as the basic tools of the researcher:

- library and information resources;
- measurement techniques;
- statistics; and
- facility with language.

The first tool enables researchers to find out what is already known in the field, the second enables them to experiment with and test new theories (hypotheses) on the basis of data they have collected, the third enables them to evaluate their results, and the fourth enables them to report these results to the scientific community. This last step adds to the pool of information available to humankind, and so becomes the start of a new cycle.

In many fields, computer hardware and software and mathematics are vital additional tools.

USING THIS BOOK

This books is in five parts, each dealing with a major element of the research process, as indicated by the title of each part.

Part 1: Getting Started
Part 1 deals with how to get started in research. First, we describe various types of research. We next present a 'research recipe', which gives the basic steps in the research process. We discuss the first two steps: finding a topic and preparing a statement of the research problem. We then describe sources of information and how to access them, emphasising the usefulness of library resources and the Internet. Finally, we outline the processes of enrolling for postgraduate study and obtaining funding.

Part 2: Data and Designs
Part 2 deals with the design of research and the collection of data. We first describe the experimental method and the role of variables. We then explain the role and use of sampling in research. We look next at the use of instruments to collect data, and how the reliability and validity of instruments can be tested. Finally, we focus on the particular problems of laboratory work, modelling and simulation, and collecting data from people.

Part 3: Statistics in Research
Part 3 deals with the analysis of data. We begin by describing how to organise, summarise and depict data. A section on regression follows, in which we describe how to fit curves to measured data. We then introduce the normal probability distribution, and show how this is used in statistical estimation. In the remainder of Part 3 we describe several statistical tests used to determine if data conforms to certain patterns.

Part 4: Research Writing

Part 4 deals with scientific writing. We begin with some suggestions for better communication, and then discuss typological usage in the writing of reports. Thereafter we describe techniques used to reference other people's work, and then conclude the part by outlining specific formats for theses, dissertations and other research reports.

Part 5: Broader Issues in Research

Part 5 deals with a number of more general research issues. We begin by discussing ethical issues in research, and the question of what constitutes intellectual honesty. Next we look at the history and philosophy of scientific research. Finally we look to the future by discussing the role of research in South Africa's reconstruction and development. We then conclude this part with some case studies showing research in practice.

Part 1

GETTING STARTED

Research sounds serious – very, *very* serious. But it can also be fun. It all depends on whether you know what you're doing or not!

As with any journey, you have to start somewhere. In this part of the book we consider the first steps in getting informed about research, the first steps in a researcher's academic career, and the first steps in a research project.

In Chapter 1 we describe various types of research. In Chapter 2 we present a 'research recipe', which gives the basic steps in the research process. We discuss the first two steps: finding a topic and preparing a statement of the research problem. In Chapter 3 we describe sources of information and how to access them. This includes exploiting the library and the information superhighway, the Internet. Finally, in Chapter 4, we outline the processes of enrolling for postgraduate study and obtaining funding.

Good luck, and have fun!

Chapter 1

Types of Research

Because the research process often draws simultaneously from several different types of research, it is useful initially to identify these types. In this chapter, therefore, we discuss the various types of research, and when they are appropriate.

1.1 EXPERIMENTAL RESEARCH

The cornerstones of science are experimental and creative research. Experimental research is primarily concerned with cause and effect. Researchers identify the variables of interest, and try to determine if changes in one variable (called the **independent variable**, or **cause**) result in changes in another (called the **dependent variable**, or **effect**). Experimental research might be used to determine if a certain material is fire-resistant or if a new teaching method achieves better results.

Some variables might be present that are neither the independent nor the dependent variable, but still need to be considered. Say we wanted to test whether a new drug was effective in reducing blood pressure in rats. The independent variable would be the use or non-use of the new drug, the dependent variable the blood pressure. However, other factors may have an effect on blood pressure: for example, the rat's genetic make-up, its weight and its stress level. To get a true answer to the question of the relationship between the independent and the dependent variable, the effect of these other factors must somehow be cancelled out. One common way to do this is to use two groups, an experimental group and a control group, which are treated identically except for the use or non-use of the drug. The design of such experiments is discussed in Chapter 5.

1.2 CREATIVE RESEARCH

Creative research involves the development of new theories, new procedures and new inventions. For example, a computer scientist might apply new algorithms for managing a computer system, an economist might develop a new model of the world economic system, or an electronic engineer might design a new radio. Creative research is used to some extent in all fields. Unlike experimental research, creative research is much less structured and cannot always be preplanned.

Creative research includes both practical and theoretical research. **Practical creative research** is about the design of physical things (artefacts) and the development of real-world processes. **Theoretical**

creative research is about the discovery or creation of new models, theorems, algorithms, etc. Practical research mainly proceeds by **trial and error.**

1.3 DESCRIPTIVE RESEARCH

Descriptive or 'case-study' research is research in which a specific situation is studied either to see if it gives rise to any general theories, or to see if existing general theories are borne out by the specific situation. An example of this is Mead's anthropological studies of isolated cultures to see whether pervasive social organisations are essential features of humankind (Lou91).

Descriptive research may be used when the object of the research is very complex. For example, in trying to study the effectiveness of health-care delivery systems, a researcher might undertake an in-depth case study of a selected number of hospitals in a selected number of countries, and then compare them to see if any general trends emerge.

1.4 *EX POST FACTO* RESEARCH

While in experimental research the researcher exposes similar groups to different treatments to see the effects of the treatments (so moving from cause to effect), in *ex post facto* research he/she looks back at the effects and tries to deduce the causes from these effects. *Ex post facto* means 'from after the fact', and this type of research typically occurs when data are available that could not be generated by experimental research. It is important to note that for *ex post facto* research to be valid, the researcher must eliminate all other possible causes.

The relationship between road development in an area and its current population would be an example. This could, of course, be experimentally tested, but few researchers have the funds to build road systems or the time to see the effects of these over 20 years!

1.5 ACTION RESEARCH

Kurt Lewin said that '[t]here's nothing so practical as a good theory' (Bar94). This idea is one of the keys to his particular approach to research, which has become known as 'action research'. As an example, if a company had a problem with absenteeism, then the steps in action research would be as follows:

1. The researcher would gather comprehensive data about both the specific problem (from the company) and the general topic (from a literature study).

2. The researcher and the stakeholders would agree on some recommendations, and these would be implemented by the company.
3. After a suitable time-period, the researcher would make pre-agreed measurements to determine the effectiveness of the changes.
   (Adapted from App91)

Some view action research as a philosophy of research rather than a method of research. They reject the attempted separation of the investigator and the problem, and instead embrace research that has the specific goal of social change, where the research is participatory and emancipatory. An example might be a community deciding on the siting of new facilities.

1.6 HISTORICAL RESEARCH

Studies of the past to find cause–effect patterns are known as historical research. It is often geared towards using past events to examine a current situation and to predict future situations (e.g. stock-market forecasting). The research does not directly study current causes or effects. Data is gathered from primary sources (i.e. records made when the past events took place) and secondary sources (i.e. records made after the events took place).

1.7 EXPOSITORY RESEARCH

This is research based purely on existing information, and normally results in 'review'-type reports. By reading widely on a field, and then comparing, contrasting, analysing and synthesising all points of view on a particular subject, a researcher can often develop important new insights. An analysis of the works of a prominent author or a comparison of the tax structures in developed and developing countries are both examples of this type of research.

Discussion Questions and Exercises

1. What type of research might be suitable for each of the following?
   a) the design of a new information systems package for doctors;
   b) an assessment of the availability of facilities for physically challenged people at sports events;
   c) the development of a vaccine against HIV/Aids;

d) an examination of the paintings of the early San people;
e) the evaluation of a new computer-based teaching technique;
f) research into the factors leading to women having fewer children;
g) research into the origins of the universe.

2. The expression 'empirical research' is used to describe the study of things as they currently exist in the real world. *Ex post facto* research is a class of empirical research, while historical research is not. Why should this be the case?

Chapter 2

Getting Started

This chapter outlines the steps in the research process, and describes in detail the initial phases of choosing a problem topic and formulating a clear research question.

2.1 A 'RESEARCH RECIPE'

The research process involves the following steps:
1. Become aware of a topic and problem.
2. Convert the problem into a well-demarcated research problem.
3. Carry out the research (using data collection or experimentation).
4. Analyse the results.
5. Write up the findings.

Steps 1 and 2 are discussed in this chapter, while steps 3 to 5 are discussed in detail later in this book.

2.2 BECOMING AWARE OF A PROBLEM

The specific subject addressed by the research is called the **topic**, while the specific question addressed in the research is called the **problem**. Finding a topic is often the first step in research, but sometimes a researcher is presented with a problem that defines the topic to be studied. For postgraduate students, finding a topic and problem can, until they are found, seem like the most important thing in their lives!

There are several sources of research problems. The most common are discussed below.

Prior Research

Studies of previous research will often suggest useful new research problems. In scientific study, the answer to a particular problem often suggests a number of new problems: 'The outcome of any serious research can only be to make two questions grow where only one grew before' (Veblen, in Coh80). For example, Mendel's early studies into heredity in plants (a translation of his original paper is given in Pet59) raised the problem of how hereditary traits are passed through generations. This generated a tremendous amount of research in the field of genetics. The understanding of how genes work is now the basis of new research into how genetic material can be altered to produce desirable results (e.g. cows that produce more milk or crops that give greater yields and resist disease).

Needs

Applied research often arises from the specific needs of industries, institutions and even countries. There are many needs, e.g. South Africa might want to find materials and designs for quality low-cost housing, a drug company might want to produce a better headache suppressant, a paint company might want to produce longer-lasting paints, a moving firm might want to minimise the total distance its trucks travel, a technikon might want to devise an exam timetable that minimises clashes.

New Opportunities

New practical and theoretical breakthroughs often open the door to new research on how these breakthroughs can be used. The manufacture of strong, lightweight alloys stimulated research in the field of aircraft design, just as the silicon chip stimulated research in the design and manufacture of more effective computers. The availability of optical technology is even now creating new possibilities in computers. Similarly, the development by Leibniz and Newton of the theory of calculus enabled researchers to solve many problems that were previously unsolvable.

Intellectual Curiosity

Some of the greatest research has resulted from someone simply sitting down and asking 'Why?' or 'How?' about something. Leonardo da Vinci asked how birds fly, and produced the first design for a flying machine. In the 1850s, Ignaz Semmelweis asked why more people die in some hospitals than in others, and as a result discovered that sterile conditions are necessary in operations (Gro95). Of course, the impulse to ask 'Why?' is fundamentally human – listen to any four-year old! But it takes some insight and some experience to ask the *right* questions.

All questions are not created equal. Great scientists choose 'good' research questions that are answerable by the methods available, and then provide useful answers. Recognising a 'good' question is largely an intuitive step based on experience and a particular mind-set. A simple example will illustrate this. Isaac Newton is reported to have begun his investigations into gravity after an apple fell on his head. His past experience (his background in mathematics), together with the experience of the event (being hit by an apple), combined with his mind-set (his interest in basic questions about the physical universe) all contributed to his choice of research question. Usually, of course, a far more complex set of experiences is involved when a researcher intuitively decides that a particular topic is 'promising' or 'unpromising'.

It should be stressed that these sources of research problems – prior research, needs, new opportunities and intellectual curiosity – are major ways in which researchers can generate ideas for topics of research. But in order to decide what a good topic in a particular field would be, the researcher must first have a substantial knowledge of the field in question and of current developments in that field (which are normally obtained by a literature study, as we will discuss in the next chapter).

2.3 PROBLEMS VERSUS RESEARCH PROBLEMS

Let's say that an electronic engineer wants to find the best way to send TV signals to a remote rural community. This is certainly a problem topic; however, the problem is not yet clearly defined. What options are there – satellite, microwave relays, land lines, others? Where precisely is the community, and what factors, if any, must be considered as a result of its particular location? (For example, a land-line service to a community in mountainous terrain would be problematic.) What has been done locally and internationally in dealing with similar problems? These questions and others like them must be answered if the engineer is to convert her problem into a scientific research problem.

In other words, a research problem should be well understood. This requires a preliminary literature survey and the identification of relevant variables. (In the example given above, the type of communication medium would be a relevant variable.) A full **demarcation** of the research problem is also necessary (demarcation is the process of setting boundaries). If you don't know the boundaries of what you're working on, you will find you have no direction to your research; or, to put it another way, if you don't know exactly *what* you are doing and exactly *why* you are doing it, it will be impossible to know *how* to do it!

2.4 WHAT SHOULD BE DEMARCATED?

The process of demarcation involves determining the scope of the study, what variables are involved, how the research will be pursued, and what practical constraints are involved.

The Scope of the Study

Do you want to investigate a general solution to a problem, or are you just interested in one that works for a particular area or field? A particular solution to our electronic engineer's problem might work for the community concerned, but might not be applicable to all remote communities. If a general solution is required, then a far wider study is needed. Similarly, a chemist creating a long-lasting paint needs to know whether the paint is required for houses in the Sahara or for cars in Alaska.

The scope of the full literature study must also be demarcated at this stage – how widely and deeply will you need to study the topic before tackling the problem? The information explosion of recent years has made it virtually impossible to read *everything* published in a particular field, but a preliminary literature study should give you a reasonable idea of what reading *is* essential. Chapter 3 gives an outline of the sources of information that are available.

Variables

A variable is any item of interest that can have more than one possible value (in other words, its value can be varied). Variables are at the heart of scientific and engineering research. At this stage of the research, the variables involved must be **identified**.

Here are some examples of variables:

If a researcher increases the temperature (variable A), what effect does this have on a guinea-pig's respiration rate (variable B)?

At what signal-to-noise ratio (variable A) is real-time voice communication practical? (Variable B here is the practicalness or not of the communication.)

How long (variable A) will 2 ml of sulphuric acid take to make a hole through cardboard of various widths (variable B)?

Variables can be either **qualitative** (i.e. they can vary between settings like practical/non-practical, absent/present or good/mediocre/bad) or **quantitative** (i.e. they can vary between numerical settings). The quantitative variables can be either **discrete** (i.e. limited to a finite number of possible settings) or **continuous** (i.e. consist of a range of real numbers).

Chapter 5 of this book, which deals with experimental design, discusses variables in more depth.

Research Methods

Next you need to specify how you will go about finding a solution or solutions to your problem, and what steps are necessary to do so. Part 2 of this book covers various research methodologies in detail.

Practical Constraints

Most research is limited by practical constraints of some kind. For example, the expected cost and duration of the research are important considerations. It is essential that a researcher knows roughly how long the research problem will take to solve, and what it will cost. There are problems that need 20 years of work, while others can be solved in months. Would you be happy studying for a particular degree if nobody could tell you how long people normally took to complete it? Having an idea of costs is also important, for no research will be practicable unless the necessary funding is available.

2.5 A STATEMENT OF THE RESEARCH PROBLEM

Having performed your preliminary study and demarcated the problem, you are now in a position to make a statement of the research problem (often referred to as the 'statement of the problem'). This statement will be the base on which your eventual report will stand, and needs to be clear and coherent. In particular the statement of the research problem will:

- ask a question or questions, normally about the relationships between variables;
- be empirically testable (i.e. testable in the real world), and moreover be testable within the time, budget, experience and resource constraints of the researcher; and
- define the potential usefulness of the result(s) of the research.
  (Adapted from Bes92)

Finally, the researcher should be *interested* in solving the problem. No one is more certain to fail than a researcher who doesn't really care about the topic he/she is researching.

Discussion Questions and Exercises

1. Dover Dairies wants to introduce a new ice-cream product and wants to know what colour the product should be to make it sell. How would you go about converting this into the statement of a research problem?

2. Discuss the difference between a problem and a research problem, and give several examples of each.

3. The city council has money to build one new railway line, and wants to know where it should go. What factors need to be considered? How would you set about posing this as a research problem?

4. Think about your favourite hobby and propose a research project that arises from it.

5. Obtain a copy of a scientific magazine (such as *Omni* or *Scientific American*), read one of the articles and suggest further research questions that stem from it.

Chapter 3

Sources of Information

In this chapter we begin by showing why the study of existing information about a field is a vital part of research. We then discuss various sources of information available to the researcher, and describe ways in which such information can be accessed. The final section emphasises the importance of note-keeping.

3.1 WHY STUDY THE PAST?

The Tragic Story of I. M. Abuvit: A Case Study

I. M. Abuvit was a postgraduate student of exceptional intelligence and diligence who had never failed in any task he attempted. On receiving a research topic from a friend in industry, he boldly stated: 'There is no way *I'm* spending months looking through boring books and journals. It's a waste of the time that would be far better spent in solving the problem.' So he immediately set about solving the problem. After a couple of false starts, where he tried approaches that didn't lead to solutions (it took four months before he discovered that they weren't going to work), he finally found a promising line of investigation. A year later he proudly presented his finished thesis, expecting accolades for completing his research in just 16 months.

But I. M. Abuvit failed miserably. The examiners noted the following flaws:

1. Both initial approaches explored by I. M. had been studied before, and there were available publications proving that the approaches would not work. I. M. had wasted four months finding out something he could have discovered in four minutes!
2. I. M.'s lack of reading had left him ignorant of some of the subtler variables involved in the problem, and he had therefore not included these in his calculations. His final results were thus incorrect.
3. Six months before he began his research, a journal had reported a successful solution to the specific problem I. M. was working on. All his research had therefore been totally unnecessary!

Unfortunately, I. M. Abuvit's story is rather common. It is *vital* to find out what other people have discovered about the field in general and about the topic in particular before you start on your own research. How solutions to related problems in the field were found can be enormously helpful in guiding research into the new problem, just as awareness of partial solutions to the new problem can save a lot of legwork. Even a so-called 'negative result', where people find that a particular approach will not work, can help you avoid blind alleys.

The expression **literature study** is often used to describe the process of finding out about previous work from a range of sources (only some of which are literary). Any good research includes two distinct types of literature study.

1. A **preliminary literature study** allows the researcher to get a feel for the topic and the issues involved, and understand how the proposed research would fit into them. This is done as preparation for research, and should precede any written proposal to conduct research (e.g. a proposal of a masters topic). One important outcome of the preliminary study is finding out what further sources need to be consulted in the full study.
2. A **full literature study** is a far more comprehensive study which is part of the research process itself rather than part of the preparation for research. The bulk of this study should be done *prior* to embarking on experimentation or data collection, so that the results of the study can be used during these activities. However, during the course of the research itself you should 'top up' your knowledge of recent developments by reading current publications.

3.2 SOURCES OF INFORMATION

The main sources of information available to researchers are:

- textbooks;
- articles in scientific journals;
- conference proceedings;
- theses and dissertations;
- company reports;
- people;
- magazines and newspapers; and
- the Internet.

The first four items on the list are the most reliable sources of information, and are the most commonly referenced in scientific reporting. We now discuss particular features of each medium.

Textbooks

Textbooks should be the starting place for finding out about a new field. The extent of detail that can be covered in a full-length book is far more than the detail that can be covered in a ten-page journal article or conference paper. Textbooks do have an inherent disadvantage, though, in that they often contain out-of-date information, particularly in fast-developing fields. This is because for most textbooks it takes at the very least a year from the time the first words are written to the time the finished product is available in published form (and usually longer), so, for example, a textbook published in 1999 will probably contain five-year-old information or worse by 2002. Using the current edition of a book (authors regularly update their books and each update becomes a new edition) helps to minimise this problem.

Articles in Scientific Journals

Journal articles are the bread-and-butter of scientific reporting. Thousands of journals exist, each publishing new work in a specific scientific field. Most journals are peer-reviewed, i.e. when an author sends a manuscript to a journal, independent experts in the field read the submission to determine whether the work reported is valid and useful or not. If it is, then the manuscript is published as a paper or article.

Different journals naturally have different standards, and the question of what constitutes a 'reputable' journal is a problematic one – people working in the field know the answer, but from outside it is not always obvious. In South Africa, an aid to the researcher is the national SAPSE list of approved journals, which is updated every year.

Articles published in reputable journals have two obvious advantages as sources of information.

1. Such articles tend to be significant as well as reliable, because, in order to be published in the journal, they have gone through the peer-review process.
2. Journal articles reflect more recent work than textbooks. So the textbook may be seen as the base for information in a field, while the journal articles provide the 'top-up' of new information as and when new results are reported.

Unfortunately, the staggering increase in scientific progress has led many prestigious journals to receive papers faster than they can publish them, and so waiting lists have become a feature in the very place where one expects to find cutting-edge results.

Conference Proceedings

Conferences are gatherings of researchers in a particular field where scientific results are presented as papers. These conferences enable established and budding researchers to interact, and also promote the rapid dissemination of the latest results of research in the field. Many conferences publish **proceedings**, which are collections of the (major) papers presented at the conference. Proceedings are a very valuable source of the most current information. A drawback is that, because many conference proceedings are not as stringently peer-reviewed as journals are, the articles may not always be as reliable.

Theses and Dissertations

Theses and dissertations are the finished product, or 'write-up', of masters and doctoral candidates. In some institutions, the term 'thesis' refers to a masters report and 'dissertation' to a doctoral one, while other institutions have it the other way around, and the rest use one of the terms for either type of report.

Masters and doctoral theses/dissertations are generally stored in the libraries of the institutions where they were presented, and are available via Interlibrary Loans (see the section entitled **The Library**, below). Apart from using these reports as reference works, postgraduate students should also check them to ensure that a topic of study hasn't already been researched. Sabinet searches that find current work being done at Southern African institutions can be useful in this regard.

Company Reports

Many companies commission scientific research into practical problems. The results of such research are typically described in a company report prepared by the researcher(s) for the company. These reports can be a valuable source of information if the company is willing to make them available – obviously, commercial or security concerns often preclude this.

People

If you know that Ntombifuthi Khumalo at the university down the road (or across the country – or across the world) is working in the field you intend researching, it makes sense to speak to her. Apart from providing useful preliminary results on the problems she is working on, she might also have useful insights into ways of tackling your problem. The key rule here is to ensure that the people you speak to are in fact experts in the field – asking the local supermarket manager for his advice on nuclear power plant design is clearly pointless and possibly dangerous.

Magazines and Newspapers

Some magazines (e.g. *National Geographic*) have strong track records of reliable reporting, while others (which we leave the reader to name) are less reliable. Magazine and newspaper reports are rarely used in research except as stepping-stones in tracking down more reliable information. Generally, a first publication of a scientific result in a magazine or newspaper (as opposed to a magazine or newspaper reporting on what has already been published in journals or conference proceedings) should be treated with great caution.

The Internet

This global network of computer networks contains many millions of files of data (including books, articles, reports and results). The Internet is an excellent way to try to track down information, but since one cannot always be sure of the correctness of the data on a site, it should not by itself be a large-scale source of information.

3.3 ACCESSING INFORMATION

There are three steps to obtaining information: finding out which reports (books, articles, etc.) are useful, obtaining copies of them, and then *reading* them. The usefulness or otherwise of the material can be determined from:

- *The title of the report.*
- *Abstracts.* Most articles and papers have brief abstracts that summarise the key points. Reading through the abstracts is a quick way to determine the relevance of the work to your own topic.
- *Work referenced by other people.* The idea here is that if you find a report particularly useful, then the sources that the writer of that report used are also likely to be useful. A list of such sources (called a 'source list,' 'reference list' or 'bibliography') normally appears at the end of a scientific report.
- *Summary publications.* In many fields there is a journal or organisation that keeps track of new works published in a particular subject and provides regularly updated summary lists.

We will next look at where one can obtain the various reports we have mentioned.

The Library

Your institution's library is always the best place to start – many postgraduates are surprised to find out the scope of resources available at their own libraries. Your subject librarian can be enormously helpful in obtaining information for you – saying 'please' and 'thank you' a great deal is highly recommended here. Apart from the books your library holds and the journals it subscribes to, you can obtain virtually any book or article in the world through your library by using a service called Interlibrary Loans. Furthermore, many libraries stock CD-ROM databases of articles in particular fields.

Your library will have facilities for searches of local and international databases such as Sabinet or DIALOG. Ask your subject librarian to explain the facilities on offer. You can search these databases for **keywords** (specific terms relevant to your topic), and you will then receive abstracts of all the papers where these keywords appear. From the abstracts, you can decide which papers you want your library to order for you. It takes some experience to ensure an effective search, which your supervisor and subject librarian can provide.

The Internet

For most people, the biggest problem in using the Internet is that there is *too much data available*, and it is very difficult to sift out useful information from irrelevant data. The various general search engines often suggest many sites that sound relevant, but turn out to be completely useless. You therefore have to find some other way of getting more focused information on the Internet.

One useful place to start is the specialised associations or societies in your particular field. Another place for getting information from the Internet is **newsgroups**. There are thousands of newsgroups, each devoted to a specific subject of interest. Apart from reading the communications of other people, you can also 'post' (send) your own contributions or questions to the group, so effectively enlisting the help of people around the world.

When you are new to a newsgroup, you should 'lurk' (i.e. just read news items) for a couple of weeks, before joining in with your own questions and comments – it is rude to 'speak' and not 'listen' whether you are communicating verbally or electronically. You can also read the list of frequently asked questions (FAQ). Most newsgroups have an FAQ list, which is designed to give new members an idea of the group's function and interests, and to answer common questions. If you waste everyone's time by posting a question that is answered in the FAQ, you can be sure of a very negative response. At best people will ignore your question (and you); more likely you will be 'flamed' (i.e. badly insulted); and in the worst-case scenario your computer could suddenly find itself flooded with 'junk' files. (This is only done to people who are *particularly* obnoxious, so there's no need to worry if you avoid being so.) The latest copies of FAQs for all newsgroups can be FTPed from an archive address such as rtfm.mit.edu (mit = Massachusetts Institute of Technology, edu = educational institution, and rtfm = read the (fine?) manual).

People

Communication with researchers in the field allows you to check progress in the field and acquire information or reports that aren't otherwise available. Such communication could be by normal mail, but it is more efficient to communicate using electronic mail (i.e. e-mail). You might obtain an author's e-mail address from an article or book, or from someone else in your field, or by using a browser on the Internet to access the electronic 'phonebook' at the author's institution.

3.4 MAKE A RECORD

The use of phrases like 'Someone I read said something like ...' in your reports will not endear you to your fellow researchers. From the start, you should keep accurate records of any information you receive by making a summary of each report. Your records should also include the information you need to reference each source (see Chapter 13 for details), i.e. the title, the author(s), the year of publication, and:
- *for books*: the publisher and place of publication;
- *for journals*: the journal name, volume and number; and
- *for proceedings*: the conference name and the place where it was held.

You must also design an efficient system to *organise* your records. If your information isn't organised, you won't be able to find information or references when you need them – and your thoughts won't be organised either!

Discussion Questions and Exercises

1. Distinguish among the eight sources of information and give the advantages of each. Can you think of some sources we have not mentioned?

2. Go to the library. Locate your subject librarian. Smile and say 'hi'.

3. Find out what databases are available for your field.
4. Get yourself connected to the Internet. Find the newsgroup for your favourite sport (probably rec.sport.yoursport) and lurk.
5. Read the FAQ for the newsgroup you found in exercise 4, above.
6. Read the South African Constitution on the Internet. (Try http://www.constitution.org.za.)
7. Browse the Internet for items concerning your academic field (e.g. quantum mechanics).

Chapter 4

Academia and Accounts

In this chapter, we consider the special case of a researcher undertaking research as part of his or her postgraduate studies.

4.1 ACADEMIA

The major academic institutions in South Africa are universities and technikons. Here you can not only do research, but also get an internationally recognised postgraduate qualification for doing it.

Traditionally, the universities have been portrayed as the bastions of pure research and the technikons the hives of applied research. In fact, in South Africa, national policies actually stated at one stage that applied research should be the domain of technikons while pure research should be that of the universities. The overlap between pure and applied research, which we briefly discussed earlier, together with the move by universities towards tackling more relevant problems, has resulted in this distinction being no longer valid (if it ever was).

Degrees

There are several degrees you can get through postgraduate study, including masters and doctorates. Traditionally, the South African masters was entirely based on one project (culminating in a thesis or dissertation). Recently, however, there has been a move towards incorporating course-work elements in the masters programme, and up to half the content may now be advanced courses in the field in which the student is working. This is in line with masters programmes in most other countries. Many institutions and faculties also offer purely course-work masters programs, but since these do not involve research, we ignore them here.

A four-year degree is generally required for entry into a masters programme, though occasionally considerable years of relevant experience will be considered as a substitute. The four-year Bachelor of Technology degree at a technikon allows entry into a Master of Technology programme. Four-year bachelor degrees (e.g. B.Sc. Engineering) or honours bachelor degrees at a university allow entry into masters programmes. A great deal of work has been done to allow easy movement of students from one institution to the other (AUT94).

The culmination of academic progress is the doctoral degree or doctorate. This is a degree that is based on a single work of research that is supposed to be a significant and original contribution to human knowledge in a particular field:

> *'A Masters degree may be thought of as a guarantee to the international community of scientists in the relevant field that they would not be wasting their time to talk to the holder. A Doctorate is a guarantee that they would not be wasting their time if they were to listen' (Mau83).*

Doctoral degrees have different titles in different institutions and fields. At technikons, a doctorate is always a D.Tech. (Doctor of Technology). Most common in universities is the Ph.D. (Doctor of Philosophy). This does *not* mean that the subject field of the doctorate was philosophy – a Ph.D. can be awarded in most subjects, e.g. engineering, science, commerce, the humanities and so on – but rather reflects the original and significant thought in the field necessary for the awarding of the degree. Field-specific names are also sometimes used for doctoral degrees, e.g. Doctor of Education. Honorary doctorates are occasionally awarded to distinguished women and men who have made major contributions to society in areas such as human rights, philanthropy and public service.

It is perhaps worth mentioning here that medical doctors who have not specialised do not in general hold doctoral degrees. To practice general medicine in South Africa you need two bachelors degrees – Bachelor of Medicine and Bachelor of Surgery (the 'Ch.' comes from the word 'chirugia', which is Latin for surgery). Society accords medical doctors with these qualifications the title 'Doctor' as a mark of respect.

Research towards a Postgraduate Degree

You need to choose an institution and a department where you want to do the research for your degree. Remember that no one department in any institution in the country is the best in all fields of a subject, since different departments have different specialisations – which usually means that they have individual staff members who specialise in particular fields in a subject. Ideally you should choose a department that has a specialist in the field you wish to research – of course, this might well be the same institution where you did your undergraduate studies.

The process of enrolling for a masters program varies from place to place. In general, you apply to the relevant faculty or department to be admitted to the program, and, depending on whether they have the necessary expertise in the field – and on the academic results you achieved in your previous degree – they accept or reject you. At some stage a formal research proposal (see **Proposals to Conduct Research** in Chapter 14) is required – some institutions require a full proposal before you actually register for a degree. You will write this proposal yourself with the aid of a mentor.

The term 'mentor' here covers supervisors, advisors and promoters. A mentor guides you through every stage of the academic process, from setting out to find a topic until the examined thesis lands on the dean's desk several years later. They are there to deal with every type of academic problem. (Have realistic expectations of them, though – while you can devote yourself fully to one research project, they may have several students and courses to teach, and will also be busy with research projects of their own.) So aim for one who is concerned about you, interested in your field, competent, has reasonable expectations, reads your drafts in a reasonable amount of time and gives consistent advice.

In addition to your departmental mentor, sometimes an additional mentor, whose specialist knowledge can contribute to your work, is appointed from outside your department, faculty or even institution. While the choice of mentor is often determined by the student's choice of area of research, it should be noted that a mentor, especially at the doctoral level, can have considerable influence on a student's career (finding jobs, writing letters of recommendation, etc.). Mentors can also become important research collaborators.

Getting a postgraduate degree can at times be hard going and frustrating. However, the eureka! experience and the pure sense of achievement you will experience will be among the greatest thrills of your life.

4.2 RESEARCH FUNDING

You will also need money. Research is often expensive. Most researchers rely on three main sources of funding – their own institutions, funding bodies and industry.

Different academic institutions have different mechanisms for funding research. These range from scholarships and paid graduate assistant posts for postgraduates, to grants and even salary subventions for staff members. Check what is available at your institution – if you don't ask, you won't get!

Two major statutory bodies fund research. The National Research Foundation (NRF) includes the old Foundation for Research Development and Centre for Science Development, and supports research in engineering, science, the humanities and commerce. The Medical Research Council (MRC) supports medical and related research. Sometimes there is an overlap of interests, e.g. an engineer working on the design of a new device for laser surgery.

These bodies offer a range of support programs that financially support specific research projects in approved areas and provide scholarships for postgraduate students. Such scholarship awards take into account the student's undergraduate results, as well as the supervisor assigned to the work. The NRF is currently providing additional support to encourage applied research and to promote research cultures at the technikons and previously disadvantaged universities.

Almost all applications for funding require a proposal for your research. This should be very carefully written and should be realistic. Asking for a million rand for a piece of equipment for the writing of one thesis will not succeed!

Discussion Questions and Exercises

1. Find out what areas your department specialises in. Then go to the same department at a neighbouring institution and find out what it specialises in.

2. Visit the website www.nrf.ac.za.

Part 2

DATA AND DESIGNS

In this part we discuss the process of actually doing research.

In Chapter 5 we discuss the design or methodology of the research. This includes the concepts of variables, controlling variables, taking samples, and experimental and control groups. In Chapter 6 we discuss the process of collecting data. We start with the design of reliable and valid instruments, and then focus on data collection in the laboratory, through the use of models or simulation. In Chapter 7 we discuss the problems of collecting data from humans.

Chapter 5

Research Design

Empirical research includes experimental, *ex post facto* and descriptive (case study) research. In this chapter we look at variables and how to control them, samples and how to take them, and other important design issues in empirical research.

5.1 INTRODUCTION

Empirical research works by the process of **induction**. Induction is the formulation of general theories from specific observations, as opposed to **deduction**, which is the derivation of a new logical truth from existing facts. As an example of induction, if you observed 500 tomatoes and found in each case that the tomato was red, you might induce that all tomatoes are red. As an example of deduction, say you know as facts that (1) all stars contain hydrogen, and (2) the sun is a star; then you can deduce the new fact that (3) the sun contains hydrogen. Note that the results of deduction are always true (if the existing facts used are true) while the results of induction are not necessarily true (some tomatoes are green!).

Almost all scientific theories are based on induction. This leads to the possibility of such theories being wrong. As a result, a theory must be continually **tested**. One inconsistent observation is enough to disprove a theory, but no amount of supporting observations can prove it absolutely – they only add to people's confidence in the theory.

Experimental research uses the **experimental method**. The experimental method can be thought of as **systematic trial and observation**: 'trial' because the answer is not known before-hand, 'observation' because the result(s) must be carefully observed and recorded, and 'systematic' because all good research is planned and purposeful.

5.2 VARIABLES

In the experimental method, the researcher chooses a **variable** (also known as a **factor**) and manipulates it. The variable that is manipulated is known as the **independent variable**. The effect of this manipulation on other variables (the **dependent variables**) is measured. Say researchers wished to study the effect of temperature (the independent variable) on the heart rates of cows (the dependent variable). A basic approach would be to change the temperature surrounding the cows, and then measure their heart rates.

Of course, other factors can also affect heart rates, e.g. the humidity, perhaps, the cows' diet or their general health. Such factors are called **nuisance variables**. Researchers must be sure that they are measuring the effect of the independent variable on the dependent variable, rather than being misled by the effects of nuisance variables. Consider the following:

> *In Saudi Arabia murderers are publicly executed. In Britain the death penalty has been abolished. Saudi Arabia has proportionately fewer murders than Britain. Therefore the death penalty is an effective deterrent to murder.*

Scientific researchers will realise that the above is not sound reasoning. While we have an independent variable (the treatment of murderers) and a dependent variable (the number of murders committed per capita), it is unclear whether the change in the independent variable is the cause of the change in the dependent one. Saudi Arabia bans alcohol for example, and many of the murders in Britain are committed by people under the influence of alcohol – the nuisance variable (i.e. alcohol availability) thus affects the dependent variable (i.e. the murders committed). Also, the dominant religions of the two countries are different, and this introduces another nuisance variable.

Controlling Nuisance Variables

A nuisance variable that is manipulated to have no effect on the dependent variable, or that has an effect that can be determined and so separated from the effect of the independent variable, is called a **controlled variable.**

Some methods you can employ to 'damp out' the effect of nuisance variables are as follows:

1. Where possible, keep the value of the nuisance variable constant (e.g. when measuring cows' heart rates, keep the humidity at 42% throughout).
2. Incorporate nuisance variables into the design of the experiment.
3. After the experiment, use a statistical technique known as **analysis of covariance** to detect the effects of nuisance variables so that these can be separated out.

We will discuss techniques for method 2 in later sections. A discussion of covariance techniques (method 3) is beyond the scope of this book: the interested reader should consult Net82, Hog93 or Fre90 for details.

Control and Experimental Groups

Experimental research often involves doing something new – the **experiment** – and comparing it with something standard – the **control.** The experiment and control are identical except for the two values of the independent variable (e.g. present/absent or high/low). This is effectively a special case of method 1, described above. The following example shows how this works:

In testing the effectiveness of a new drug for headaches, the control group receives a placebo (a pill that has no medical effect) and the experimental group receives the actual drug, but both groups are otherwise treated the same. Usually they are not told which group they are in. This is known as a ***blind test.*** *In a* ***double-blind*** **test,** *not even the doctors dispensing the drug know whether it is a placebo or not.*

A number of nuisance effects can be cancelled out in this way. The effect of people psychologically 'feeling better' after taking medicine and the effect of changes in outside conditions during the course of the experiment (from weather conditions to the state of the economy) should be felt equally by both groups. Any difference in the groups with regard to the dependent variable (i.e. the presence and severity of headaches) can therefore be attributed to the independent variable (i.e. the use or non-use of the new drug).

Sampling and **matching** are important concepts in the design of control and experimental groups. We will discuss these concepts in the following sections.

5.3 SAMPLING

Here we introduce the concepts of a **population** and a **sample**, and discuss the 'why' and 'how' of taking scientifically useful samples.

Populations and Samples

A **population** is any group that is the subject of research interest. Oxygen molecules in the universe, supercomputers in the world, frogs in South African rivers or the dogs in a particular city could all be populations, i.e. groups a researcher wants to study.

It is often not practical or possible to study an entire population, e.g. someone trying to determine the average length of adult frogs in South Africa would find it impossible to do this by measuring each and every frog in the entire country! In such cases it is necessary to make general findings based on a study of only a subset of the population. Such subsets are called **samples.**

Samples must be **representative** of the population being studied, otherwise no general observations about the population can be made from studying the sample. A study of the incidence of mange in dogs in a city based on a sample of only puppies is unlikely to produce meaningful results. Two key features of samples determine how representative of the population they are, these being **size** and **bias**.

Sample Size

Say a gambler is playing a game of dice, and believes that one die is 'loaded', i.e. it has been weighted so that the number 1 appears more often than the other numbers. She decides to roll the die a number of times (which becomes the sample of rolls of the die) to test whether it does in general favour the number 1 (in the infinite population of rolls of the die). If she rolls the die once and gets a 1, she could say that on 100% of tests the die came up 1. However, most people would have problems accepting that just one roll is a valid test of the die. If she rolls it 5 000 times and gets a 1 every time, then most people would be convinced that the die was in fact loaded.

As the above example shows, the sample must be **large enough** to correctly represent a population. Chapter 9 gives the statistical details on how to determine what size sample is necessary to test a population correctly.

Sample Bias

Many newspapers hold 'phone-ins' in which people's views on particular topics are requested. Then some people phone in their views, and a selection of responses is published the next day. These responses are normally prefaced with editorial comments on the lines of 'People in Soweto overwhelmingly rejected ...' or 'Durbanites generally support ...'. Many people do not realise that this is complete nonsense. Think about it for a moment – who would participate in such phone-ins? People who don't read that particular newspaper? Not likely. People who don't have telephones? Not likely. People who don't have strong views on the subject? Not likely. People who are naturally shy and retiring? Again, not likely. So, in fact, these newspaper surveys are not testing the population of people in their city, but are in fact testing the population of people in the city who read the specific newspaper on the day the phone-in topic was presented, who own telephones, who are confident enough to phone in their opinions, and who are interested enough in the topic to take the time to phone in.

This example gives just some of the more obvious problems in the sampling method employed. Similar questions must be asked when 'researchers' do 'man-in-the-street' opinion testing – which man? And what street?

A sample is said to be **biased** if it represents only a specific subgroup of the population or if particular subgroups are over- or under-represented in it. The next section describes how to avoid bias.

Sampling Methods

Random selection is the basic principle used to try to avoid bias in a sample. The random selection of the sample *must* ensure that each member of the population has as much chance as any other of being included in it. So taking a sample of Bloemfontein adults by randomly selecting names from the telephone book would be biased, because people who don't have telephones do not have an equal chance of being in the sample, whereas taking a sample of students at the University of Fort Hare by randomly selecting student records would not be biased, because all registered students would have an equal chance of being selected.

We will now discuss three standard random sampling techniques.

Simple Random Sampling

Here the researchers first assign numbers to each member of the population (i.e. they **enumerate** the population). For example, people's I.D. numbers could serve as numbers for a study of South African adults, if everyone had an I.D. After performing this enumeration, the researchers generate as many unique random numbers as the size of sample required, and the corresponding members of the population become the sample. Random numbers can be generated by a computer, either by using special computer programs or the random functions available in programming languages such as Basic, Pascal and C.

Such enumeration is ideal; but it is, of course, not always possible, and other methods must be used. (The population of oxygen molecules would take quite some time to enumerate, even if it stayed constant!)

Stratified Random Sampling

Sometimes researchers have prior information regarding certain characteristics of the population's composition, and they want the selection of sample items to reflect this. For example, if they were studying housing construction in South Africa, and the population of interest was houses in the country, they might know certain rough proportions of housing types – 30% informal, 50% brick, 15% cement and 5% wood, for example. A simple random sample would be unlikely to arrive at exactly these proportions (think about it). In stratified random sampling, researchers use simple random sampling within each **group** (or **stratum**), ensuring that appropriate numbers are selected from each group so that the overall sample reflects each group in the known proportions.

To continue our example, if the researchers wanted a sample of 1 000 houses, they would select 300 informal houses randomly, then 500 brick houses, 150 cement houses and finally 50 wooden ones. Stratified random sampling is preferable to simple random sampling if members within each stratum are fairly similar (or **homogeneous**), but there are marked differences between members of one stratum and those of another.

Cluster Sampling

Simple random sampling can be impossible in large populations. It can also be economically unviable. Say researchers wished to determine the average level of toxins in South African streams, and have the time and resilience to actually enumerate all the streams in the country. A simple random sample of 200 streams would probably have them flying and driving over great distances to individual streams to measure toxin levels, and this travel would be extremely expensive as well as extremely time-consuming.

In cluster sampling, the researchers subdivide the population into subgroups called **clusters**. They then randomly select a sample of clusters, and then randomly select members of the cluster sample to serve as the population sample.

For example, they might break their South African stream population into geographically separate clusters, with each of the nine provinces forming one cluster. They could then randomly select, say, three provinces and perform simple random sampling within each province. Cluster sampling can be done on more than one level, e.g. in each of the selected provinces (clusters), they could enumerate all the magisterial districts (subclusters), and randomly select a sample of districts from which the actual sample of streams is taken. Eventually, they would be able to take their sample of 200 streams by travelling to, say, only three provinces, and to only four districts within each province, rather than having to travel to 200 completely separate locations.

Note that clusters are different from the strata of stratified random sampling. A population is divided into strata so that each stratum is defined by a known characteristic, whereas the division into clusters is based on spatial separation alone.

Cluster sampling is not quite as reliable as simple random sampling or stratified random sampling, but is often the only approach possible. A more detailed treatment of these issues is available in Coc77.

5.4 MATCHING

The placement of participants into the control or experiment group can be performed at random, and if the sample size is large enough, this should be effective. Another common approach is called **matching**. Here, say the researchers want experimental and control groups of 40 people (or dogs, or crystals) each, making a total of 80 sample items. They select the 80 sample items by random sampling, but then, instead of randomly assigning each sample item to a group to make up the two groups, they instead find sample pairs that are in some way(s) similar, and randomly assign one member of each pair to the experimental group and the other to the control group. Matching can be extremely useful if the sample size must be small and there is therefore a risk that the effects of nuisance variables will be pronounced in one group and not in the other.

Here is an example of matching. A pharmaceutical firm employs 200 trainee scientists in its research section. A new training course has been developed to teach certain skills, and the company wishes to determine if this course will be more effective than the existing one. The effectiveness will be measured by an end-of-course test. The company decides to do an experiment with a random sample of 20 scientists, with 10 taking the old course (the control group) and the other 10 taking the new course (the experimental group). However, age is known to affect how easily people absorb new knowledge, and the company wants to eliminate this nuisance variable. The staff members carrying out the research therefore divide the 20 into two groups by creating pairs according to age – the two oldest scientists as one pair, the third and fourth oldest as the next, and so on, down to the two youngest. One member of each pair is then put randomly in the control group and the other in the experimental group, so that the effects of age are felt equally between the groups, and do not contribute to any differences observed between the two groups' success.

5.5 EXPERIMENTAL DESIGN

One of the simplest experimental designs is the one involving an experimental group and a control group. However, if you have more than one independent variable, and you want to determine the effect of each independent variable on the dependent variable, then you will need a more complex design.

One such type of design is the **factorial experiment**. (Remember that the term 'factor' is another name for a variable.) In a factorial design, the researchers take each independent variable (or controlled variable) and select several levels for each. Then they try all possible combinations. For example, the researchers interested in the effect of surrounding temperature on the heart rates of cows might decide that the humidity and breed of cows are two nuisance variables that they need to control. So a simple factorial experiment might try two different breed of cows, three levels of humidity, and five levels of temperature, the result being 30 readings.

To analyse the data collected in a factorial experiment, researchers need advanced statistical techniques that are not covered in this book. So if you intend to use such a design, you should consult a book on experimental design such as Mea88 or Hic93. Also, in many situations researchers cannot afford to try each possible level of each variable. So there are more complicated designs that try to extract the same information but using fewer measurements. Again, a book on experimental design is your best guide as to how to do this.

Empirical research can also deal with changes over time. Such research can sometimes be categorised as having a **cross-sectional**, **longitudinal** or **time-lag** design. Say we are studying children's attitudes to homework. In a **cross-sectional** design we could compare the attitudes of 10-, 12- and 14-year-olds. In a **longitudinal** design we could take 10-year-olds and see how their attitudes change as they age over four years. In a **time-lag** design we could, over a four-year period, determine the attitudes of each year's 10-year-olds.

These designs can be used together. A researcher studying whether younger children are keener on homework by using a longitudinal design could find that this seems to be true. However, changes to society could have affected all children over the period of the study, e.g. the introduction of television, video games and personal computers. By using a time-lag design combined with a longitudinal design, the researcher would become aware of the effects of the nuisance variables.

Discussion Questions and Exercises

1. What is bias? How should sampling be conducted to avoid bias?

2. Suppose you used a greenhouse that keeps temperatures constant to investigate the amount of water needed to grow tomatoes using a particular fertilizer. What is/are:

a) the independent variable(s);
b) the dependent variable;
c) some possible nuisance variables;
d) the controlled variable(s)?

3. What type of sampling would you use for the following investigations and why?
   a) the tusk size of African elephants;
   b) whether rugby or soccer is more popular in South Africa;
   c) the average age of your family (think carefully about this one!);
   d) the average weight of Isaac Williams' 1 000 cows.

4. Can you estimate the quality of diamonds in the world by sampling only from Kimberley? What about the composition of diamonds?

5. Unmetricated Manufacturers has built prototypes of two different robotic car-painters. They wish to test which is faster on average. They have a sample of ten cars, with surface areas in square feet of 120, 110, 140, 230, 190, 130, 120, 150, 200, 100. Use matching to design a control group and an experimental group. How appropriate is the design?

Chapter 6

Data Collection

In this chapter, we first discuss the concepts of reliability and validity of data-measurement devices. We then describe methods of obtaining data from laboratory experiments and models. In the following chapter we explore the problems of obtaining data from people.

6.1 INSTRUMENTS

Researchers have to measure data somehow. Any device they use for this measurement is called an **instrument** (e.g. a thermometer to measure temperature, a voltmeter to measure potential difference, an I.Q. test to measure intelligence, etc.).

There are two fundamental criteria for instruments:

- reliability; and
- validity.

The term **reliability** means that measurements made are consistent, i.e. if the same experiment is performed under the same conditions, the same measurements will be obtained. The term **validity** means that the measurements are correct, i.e. the instrument measures what it is intended to measure, and that it measures this correctly.

- *Example 1*: Every month a househusband has 12 kg of fish delivered to his home. The fish is packed in ice-filled cartons to ensure freshness. He diligently weighs each delivery to ensure that he is getting the right amount of fish, and every month the scale measures 12 kg exactly. While the scale seems reliable, the measurements are not valid, as he is weighing the fish together with the packaging and the ice.
- *Example 2*: A particularly controversial issue is the use of I.Q. tests to measure intelligence. One problem with an I.Q. test is that people do not consistently obtain the same scores. The I.Q. measured varies according to people's moods, the conditions under which the test is written, people's health and many other factors. Questions therefore arise as to the reliability of I.Q. tests.

  Even if I.Q. tests were reliable (i.e. someone always got the same score), serious questions have been raised about the validity of these tests. Do I.Q. tests in fact measure intelligence? Some say that I.Q. tests simply measure how skilled people are at solving the specific types of questions asked in I.Q. tests! (See Cur90 and Jor89.)

6.2 LABORATORY WORK

When you were an undergraduate, you probably did some practical work. There were (we hope) three goals to this activity:

- learning about practical work;
- becoming familiar with a certain instrument, apparatus or technique; and
- demonstrating theory by specific experiments.

In postgraduate study, you are likely to have to deal with apparatus you have never seen before, while performing experiments where nobody knows what is supposed to happen. You may also be called upon to design and build apparatus yourself. Nonetheless, all the principles of undergraduate experiments still apply. These are laid out below.

- *Plan your work.* Before you do anything, decide what you are going to do, how you are going to do it, and how you will measure what has occurred.
- *Keep full records.* You *must* record all data accurately in a notebook. State the date, the conditions, the experimental steps and the results. Don't be vague. Diagrams can be useful!
- *Avoid obvious errors.* Most errors can be avoided by good technique, i.e. by being careful and methodical. Look for places where errors can occur. One problem is conditions changing while you are performing a series of comparative experiments. For example, in measuring the elasticity of a spring by using a series of weights, successive weights might stretch the spring and so actually alter its elasticity. Use theoretical calculations to check that various outcomes during the experiment make sense.
- *Estimate remaining inaccuracy.* You must treat data circumspectly. Often data has **noise**, i.e. inaccurate measurements amongst the accurate ones. If you cannot completely eliminate noise, then you must try to estimate the error in your results.
- *Try various alternatives.* Try alternative measuring devices or doing things in alternative orders. Apart from providing a check of the reliability of your results, differences amongst such alternatives could suggest new research problems.
- *Work safely.* Always take appropriate safety precautions, and use your common sense.

Where possible, an experiment should be repeated several times under several conditions. This is particularly true of laboratory experiments (Squ85). For results to be accepted, they must be **reproducible**, i.e. other researchers in the field should be able to read your report and from that perform similar experiments that yield similar results.

6.3 MODELLING AND SIMULATION

Models

Many problems can be **formulated** or translated into **models.** A **system** is a subset of the world that is considered to be self-contained. A **model** is a simplified representation of a system. Armed with a suitable model, researchers may try either or both of:

- mathematical analysis to solve problems about a system or optimise its functioning; and
- computer simulation to approximate what happens when it is functioning.

There are several good reasons for using a model.

1. It would be too expensive to build the real thing to see if it works (e.g. a petrochemical plant).
2. The real system exists but cannot be experimented on (e.g. a nuclear reactor).
3. Researchers can use the model for 'what-ifs' (e.g. 'what will happen to sales if the price is increased?').
4. People can use the model for forecasting (e.g. a change in the global climate).

Sometimes just designing the model is in itself a worthwhile goal, for it can provide a tool for other researchers to use, e.g. a model to aid our understanding of superconductivity (and explain high-temperature ceramics). More often, however, the model is just a first step in solving a problem.

Modelling is often used as a research tool because it can be inexpensive. Paradoxically, one limitation is cost, since computer time is not free. Other difficulties include designing a sufficiently accurate model, and the validation of the results (even if you 'know' the answer is correct, you have to justify this to others).

McHaney (McH91) states that 'the best approach to model development is to incorporate the *least amount of detail* while *still maintaining veracity*' (our emphasis). Clogging up a model or simulation with fine details can add a lot of time to the development process and such details can introduce their own problems. On the other hand, *essential detail* cannot be omitted if the model is to represent the real-world situation validly.

Simulation

The process of model creation and usage encapsulates the scientific method in miniature. The steps in a simulation are as follows:
1. Define the system and the objectives.
2. Determine the model's scope and scale (what's in it and how much detail will be included).
3. Choose a programming language and code the model.
4. Run the model.
5. Gather data and analyse it.

An example of a model is Volterra's rabbit-and-fox model of the relationship between predator and prey in a specific area (McH91).

The model is based on the fact that the greater the number of foxes, the more rabbits are eaten. Say one starts with a large number of foxes and few rabbits. In a situation such as this, the rabbit population decreases. After a while the scarcity of rabbits means that there is not enough food for the foxes, so some of the foxes die and the fox population decreases. This decrease in the fox population allows an increase in the rabbit population, which in turn leads to an increase in the fox population, and a new cycle begins.

This model:
- uses numeric calculations to predict behaviour over time, as the number of foxes at any given time is used in the calculation of the number of rabbits in the next period, and vice versa; and
- is a simplified representation of the system, since the presence of other predators and prey, as well as other ways in which foxes and rabbits could die, are not included.

Another example is the study of a queuing system. Consider a bank with several customers queuing for the next available teller. Simulation can be used to determine the behaviour of the system (e.g. the length of each customer's wait) as more and more customers are added.

The maxim 'garbage in, garbage out' applies particularly to simulations. If the input data is not truly representative of the real world, the simulation will be useless.

Writing Simulations

A simulation can be written in a standard computer language, such as C or PASCAL. There are also many special simulation languages, such as SLAM and GPSS/H, which have built-in commands and structures for some of the common situations researchers may encounter.

Software simulators are also available for specific fields. If your problem involves a situation that a simulator correctly models, the software package can obviously be enormously helpful in your research. On the other hand, if your problem has specific features that the simulator is not equipped to deal with, then it is a mistake to try to change the problem to fit the simulator.

The result of a simulation can be just a number, or even a simple yes/no to the question of, for example, whether a spaceship reaches the moon. But it is much more useful to have intermediate data displayed, preferably through the use of animation (since the eye is the best input mechanism we have). The commercial simulation languages and simulators have graphical commands built into them. Beware of proof by picture, however – a neat graphic showing the spaceship landing on the moon does *not* by itself guarantee that there is no bug in the simulation and that the real version won't explode on take-off.

Discussion Questions and Exercises

1. What criteria would you use for assessing the worth of a research instrument? Discuss.

2. Take one example of a research interest, list some of the problems of collecting data, and suggest ways to avoid them.

3. Construct a model of a student's success in a course. (Will the student pass or fail?)

4. How would you go about experimenting on:
   a) the ability of mice to find their way through a maze; and
   b) the colour of metals when burning?

Chapter 7

Data from People

In this chapter, we discuss techniques of collecting data from people. The computer analyst wanting to study user satisfaction after introducing a new system, the psychiatrist wanting to determine the stress levels of executives and the bioengineer wanting to determine the acceptability of a meat substitute all need data from people.

7.1 INSTRUMENTS

Just as you would use a barometer to measure air pressure or a stopwatch to measure time, so researchers need some instrument to measure whatever it is about people they are studying. The most common instruments they use for this purpose are tests, interviews and questionnaires.

The design of a reliable instrument for measuring people's attitudes or capabilities requires careful planning. The reliability can be checked by using one of three approaches.

1. **The test-retest approach**. In this approach, researchers administer the same instrument at a later time and see if they get the same results. However, many respondents (i.e. the people answering the questions) are not happy answering the same questions twice, and the time lag needed between test and retest can also cause responses to change and respondents to be 'lost'.
2. **The equivalent-form approach**. Each question on the original test, interview or questionnaire is rephrased so that the researchers wind up with two tests that 'look different' but effectively ask the same questions. If there is a high correlation between people's responses to the original questions and to the rephrased questions, this indicates that the test is reliable, and that people aren't just 'answering at random'.
3. **The split-half approach**. This is a modification of the equivalent form method, where the two tests (the original and the equivalent form) are combined into one. The fact that question 14 and question 87 are differently worded versions of the same question will escape most respondents' notice, and this allows the test to be given at a single sitting rather than being spread over two sessions.

Ease of use has a major impact on the reliability of instruments – as you can imagine, frustrated, bored or confused people cannot be relied on to answer a set of questions consistently – and it also ensures higher participation.

An instrument is **reliable** if it consistently gives the same results – so a calculator consistently getting an answer of 3 when it adds 2 and 2 is reliable. This does not, however, make the answer **valid** (i.e. right)! Testing the validity of a new instrument used for people is not easy. Three approaches are used; in order of preference, these are as follows:

1. **Criterion-related validity**. This measures whether an instrument accurately predicts (**predictive validity**) or diagnoses (**concurrent validity**) some particular variable (**criterion**). For example, an aptitude test for trainee mechanics could be shown to be valid if the test scores correlate highly with the respondents' eventual success or failure as mechanics. Of course, if you have an existing instrument that measured the same thing and you know that it is valid, you could simply compare the results obtained from the new instrument with those of the old. (A new test might be desirable if, for example, the current instrument is too long.)
2. **Construct validity**. If you have an existing instrument that measures something that is known to be closely related to the thing you want to measure, compare the results obtained by the new instrument with that of the old, and check that there is a high correlation. For example, say you have an existing way to measure writing skills, and your new instrument seeks to measure reading skills. If you know that reading skills are correlated with writing skills, then a high correlation between the results obtained by the new test on reading skills and the existing one on writing skills would suggest that the new test is valid.
3. **Content validity**. If no related instruments exist, then gather expert opinion on each question on the instrument to determine whether or not it actually tests what it is supposed to. In addition, the experts must agree that the questions as a whole constitute a valid and representative test of the variable being measured.

A more detailed treatment of the reliability and validity of instruments for people is available in Huy87 and Mul87.

7.2 QUESTIONNAIRES

A questionnaire is a printed list of questions that respondents are asked to answer. These instruments are commonly used – and commonly abused. It is easy to compile a questionnaire; it is not easy to compile an effective one. Effectiveness requires planning beforehand to ensure that the data can be objectively analysed afterwards.

Open (or unstructured) questions can be used in a preliminary survey or to get a feel for the subject. Here respondents answer questions in their own words. Closed (or structured) questions are used in large-scale data collection. Here respondents choose from a collection of alternatives (e.g. true/false) or assign a numerical score or ranking. Closed questions often use a four-point scale, for example:

Q12. Bart Simpson is a good role model.

Strongly disagree ☐ *Disagree* ☐ *Agree* ☐ *Strongly agree* ☐

A **four-point scale** forces a decision, while a **five-point scale** provides the possibility of a neutral answer.

A good questionnaire:

- is complete, i.e. gets all the data you need;
- is short, i.e. doesn't abuse the respondents' time or concentration;
- asks only relevant questions;
- gives clear instructions;
- has precise, unambiguous and understandable questions;
- has objective questions, i.e. doesn't suggest answers;
- starts with general questions;
- has appropriate questions;
- puts sensitive questions at the end; and
- uses mostly closed questions, often with a four-point scale.

You have no right to expect total honesty. Some participants will not care that much about an answer or will try to give a 'socially correct' answer. These problems can be reduced if you make the instrument easy to use, and explain the importance of the research to your respondents. Be courteous, thank people for their help, offer to share the conclusions with them, provide a stamped, self-addressed envelope for them to return the questionnaire.

A particular problem with questionnaires is that of **non-returns**. If you get 800 returned questionnaires from 1 000 you've distributed (which is a very high return rate), what do you do about the missing 200 responses? Unfortunately, you *cannot* just rely on the 800 that did respond to form a big enough sample, as there is the problem of bias. The particular bias involved is determined by people's reasons for not returning the questionnaire (too disorganised? too lazy? offended by the questionnaire? didn't understand it? their area didn't receive it?).

This problem with questionnaires is a specific case of the general problem with human volunteers. The fact that volunteers are unlikely to be representative of a population (more adventurous? poorer?) means that studies using volunteers are open to criticism. Studies on human sexuality have been particularly criticised in this regard (Lou91).

7.3 INTERVIEWS

An interview involves a one-on-one verbal interaction between the researcher and a respondent. Much of what was said above for questionnaires is true for interviews. An interview should have a plan. The researcher must not direct the respondent's answers through his/her tone of voice or through the way he/she phrases a question, e.g. 'You agree with us that this is right, don't you?'

One area where researchers would need to use interviews rather than questionnaires would be in getting information from people who can't read. Other advantages of an interview over a questionnaire are that the researcher can ask the respondent to clarify unclear answers and can follow up on interesting answers. Some advantages of a questionnaire over an interview are that the respondents can answer the questionnaire at times that are suitable to them, and the respondents may not be as inhibited in answering sensitive questions. However, a questionnaire is the only practical approach when dealing with many respondents.

7.4 ETHICAL CONSIDERATIONS

Apart from instrumentation and procedural concerns, collecting data from people raises ethical concerns. These include taking care to avoid harming people, having due regard for their privacy, respecting them as individuals and not subjecting them to unnecessary research.

In order to avoid harming people, you must guard against both physical and psychological harm. People have a right to privacy, and the researcher must keep collected data confidential. This implies that the subject(s) should not be identifiable to anyone reading the eventual report. Most importantly, the researcher must remember that the subjects are individual human beings, and treat them with appropriate respect. These and related questions are discussed further in Chapter 15.

Discussion Questions and Exercises

1. How would you design an instrument to test:
   a) the height of adults;
   b) the intelligence of adults;
   c) the intelligence of babies;
   d) the attitude of elderly people to changes in technology; and
   e) the racial attitudes of urban dwellers?

2. Suppose you wanted to use an aptitude test in South Africa that had been produced in the United States of America. Suggest some changes that might be needed.

Part 3

STATISTICS IN RESEARCH

Much of a researcher's time is spent accumulating and analysing data, e.g. data about temperatures, occurrences, concentrations, durations, etc. The field of **statistics** deals with the analysis of data.

Any researcher almost always has imperfect data about a small subset (i.e. the sample) of the intended population. The data is **imperfect** because of experimental, recording and other errors. The researcher has data only about a **subset** of the population because, as we saw earlier, it is impossible to examine the entire population. A botanist who proposes a law of genetics can only test this law on a tiny fraction of the plants on the planet (to say nothing about those plants not yet growing); at some stage the researcher has to stop testing and conclude that the patterns found in the sample are also found in the whole population.

We discussed in the previous chapters how to find a suitable sample. In the chapters on statistics that follow, we examine how to analyse the sample data and draw conclusions. This is known as **statistical inference**.

These chapters proceed as follows. We start with data and how to organise it in Chapter 8. We then look at probability and probability distributions in Chapter 9, especially the normal distribution. This brings us to the main purpose of Part 3: explaining estimation and statistical tests. These are used to answer questions about how confidently a researcher can extrapolate from the sample data, and whether the sample data agrees with a preconceived theory. We deal with these processes in Chapters 10 and 11.

In this book, we examine only the kinds of situations a researcher is most likely to encounter. If you need more information, then you should look in a book about statistics (e.g. Net82, Hog93, Fre90, Moo85, Mul87, Wad90) or ask a friendly statistician. A computer statistics package can also be useful, both for performing the necessary calculations and for representing the data in various ways. An example of a full statistics package is the SAS program, while more modest packages include SPSS and Minitab. A spreadsheet program such as QuattroPro, Excel or Lotus 1-2-3 can also be useful.

Chapter 8

Basic Statistics: Data Organisation

In this chapter we introduce common statistical measures and discuss the representation and organisation of data. The chapter concludes with a discussion of regression, which is a technique for fitting curves to data.

8.1 STATISTICAL MEASURES

Data can be **qualitative** or **quantitative**. **Quantitative data** has numerical values, e.g. in the range 0 to 100. **Qualitative data** has values that fall into categories, e.g. animal, vegetable or mineral. For example, whether it rained or not yesterday is a qualitative question (the categories are 'rained' and 'not rained'); how much rain fell is a quantitative question. Quantitative data can be **discrete** or **continuous**: discrete if it takes on only whole values, and continuous if it takes on any real value in some interval. The amount of rain that fell yesterday is continuous data; the number of days it rained last year is discrete data.

A **statistical measure**, or simply a **statistic**, is a summary of the data. This data can be for the entire population or for the chosen sample. We will now discuss some population statistics.

Measures of Central Tendency

Most statistics of quantitative data are either measures of **central tendency** (where the data is centred) or measures of **dispersion** (how spread out the data is). In the former category are the **mean**, the **median** and the **mode**.

The population **mean** is the average and is denoted by the Greek letter μ. If the population data values are $x_1, x_2, \ldots, x_n$, then:

$$\mu = \frac{1}{n}\sum_{x=1}^{n} x_i$$

The symbol $\sum$ (pronounced 'sigma') means 'the sum of', so the above formula says that

$$\mu = \frac{x_1 + x_2 + x_3 + \ldots + x_n}{n}$$

The **median** is the middle value if the data is sorted from smallest to biggest. If there is an even number of values, then the median is usually taken to be the average of the middle two values. The **mode** is the most common value(s) in the data.

Example: For the data 5, 3, 6, 7, 5, 5, 9, 1, 17, 9
the mean is 6.7
the median is 5.5
the mode is 5

(NOTE: In this book we use the decimal point in real numbers instead of the decimal comma, i.e. 5.42 rather than 5,42.)

While the mean is more commonly used, the median can be a better summary of the data if there are extreme values involved. For example, in statistics on the price of houses in an area, the median is often the best summary of the house prices, since the mean can be strongly influenced by one extremely high or low price. Say the selling prices in thousands of rands were 100, 100, 110, 120, 130, 140 and 980. The mean here is 240 and the median is 120. The median is a better summary, as most people paid around R120 000 for their houses.

For qualitative variables (e.g. colour) the mode is the only possible measure. For ranked data (e.g. 1st, 2nd, 3rd) both the median and the mode are possible, but the median is preferable as it considers the rankings rather than just frequencies.

Measures of Dispersion

When summarising quantitative data, a researcher is also interested in measures of dispersion, i.e. how spread out the data is. Examples of these are the **range**, **percentiles**, the **variance** and the **standard deviation**.

One simple statistic is the **range**, i.e. the gap between the largest and smallest values. This is seldom useful, as there can be eccentric data. For example, the annual incomes of South Africans range from zero to many millions of rands. However, the spread of incomes has very few people at the top extreme and very many at the bottom, and most incomes lie in a much narrower range.

One is more likely to use **percentiles**. For example, the 90th percentile is the value below which 90% of the data lies. In this terminology, the median is the 50th percentile.

Another measure of dispersion is the **variance**. The variance of the population is denoted by σ^2. This is defined as the **average squared deviation**. If the data values are $x_1, x_2, \ldots, x_n$, then

$$\sigma^2 = \frac{1}{n}\sum_{i=1}^{n} (x_i - \mu)^2$$

The (positive) square-root of the data is called the **standard deviation** of the data; the population standard deviation is denoted by σ.

Example: For the data 5, 3, 6, 7, 5, 5, 9, 1, 17, 9 (with $\mu = 6.7$)
the range is 16
the variance is 17.21
the standard deviation is 4.15

One property of the mean and the standard deviation is that if the data comes from a 'reasonable' population (this term will be defined later), then about 68% of the data lies between $\mu - \sigma$ and $\mu + \sigma$ (i.e. within one standard deviation of the mean), while 95% of the data lies within two standard deviations of the mean.

8.2 THE GRAPHICAL REPRESENTATION OF DATA

Sometimes a picture like a graph explains the situation much more clearly than a jumble of numbers. However, do not include a picture just to impress people: pictures should be relevant and useful. There are several common types of pictures, e.g. graphs, pie charts, etc. Spreadsheets and many other computer packages contain inbuilt graphing functions.

Depicting Qualitative Data

A common device for displaying qualitative data is a **pie chart**. For example, if 60% of a country's music exports is kwaito, 25% rock and 15% rap, then this could be depicted by the pie chart in Figure 1.

Figure 1: An example of a pie chart

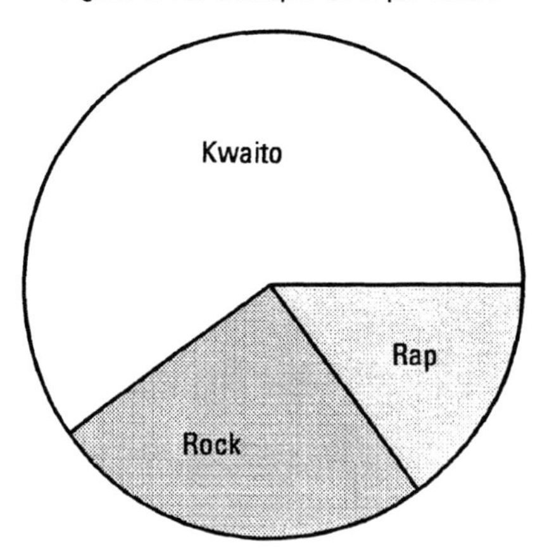

Depicting Frequency Data

In **frequency data** you divide the range of values into intervals, and count the number of data items that lie in each interval. For example, examination scores are given as a mark out of 100, and a school teacher records the number of A-plus scores (90–99%), A scores (80–89%), B scores (70–79%), C scores (60–69%), etc. The result is known as a **frequency distribution.** An example of a frequency distribution is given in Table 1.

Table 1: An example of frequency data

Interval	Frequency	Cumulative frequency	Cumulative percentage
30–39	1	1	1.56
40–49	6	7	10.94
50–59	14	21	32.81
60–69	17	38	59.38
70–79	16	54	84.38
80–89	8	62	96.88
90–99	2	64	100

A **histogram** is used to depict a frequency distribution in which the intervals have equal size. In a histogram, for each interval one draws a rectangular bar with the base of the bar the range of that interval and the height equal to the numbers recorded. Figure 2a, on the next page, shows a histogram for the discrete data given in Table 1.

You can also depict the data with a **frequency polygon.** Here the researcher plots for each interval a point above the midpoint of each interval giving the number of data items recorded, and then joins up consecutive plots, as in Figure 2b, on the next page. Note that the frequency polygon starts and ends at zero: it is assumed that the intervals immediately before and after those given both have 0 data items.

In an **ogive** the researcher looks at the data cumulatively. For each interval she calculates the cumulative count (or percentage), i.e. the number of data items up to and including that interval. Then for each interval she plots a point at the maximum of the interval giving the cumulative count (or percentage). These points are then joined up to form the ogive. (If the data is discrete, then the end of an interval is halfway between the maximum of that interval and the minimum of the next interval. So, in our example, the ends are 39.5, 49.5, etc.) The ogive increases from 0 to total count (or 100%), and is often S-shaped. An example is presented in Figure 2c, on the next page.

Figure 2a: An example of a histogram

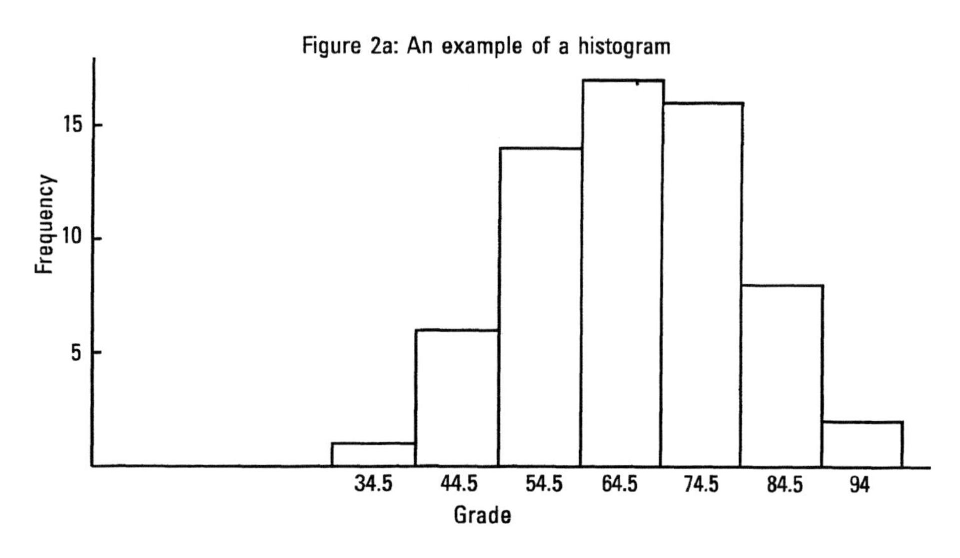

Figure 2b: A frequency polygon

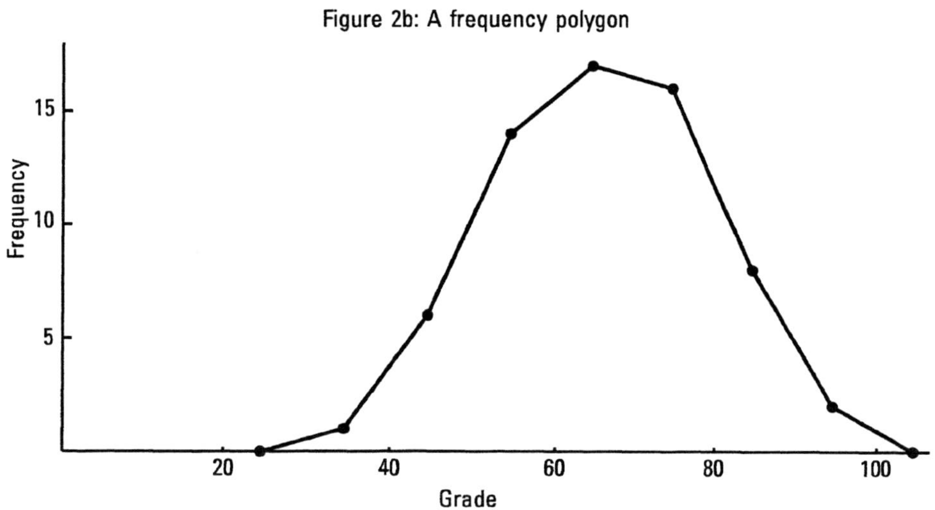

Figure 2c: An ogive

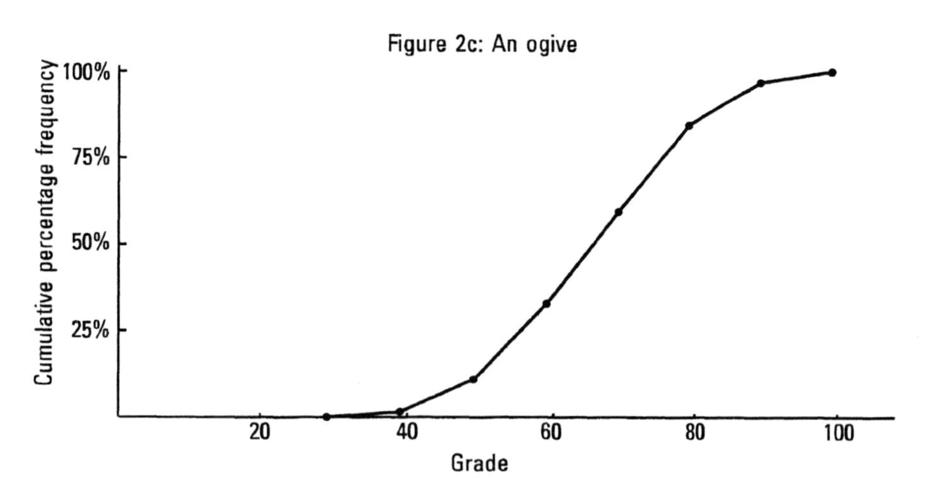

An ogive is also useful in calculating percentiles. For example, if you want to know the 70th percentile, you draw a horizontal line from 70% on the y-axis and determine where it intersects the ogive. The corresponding value on the x-axis is the percentile you are looking for.

Another simple device is a **box-and-whiskers diagram**. This gives five statistics of the data: the minimum, the maximum, the median, the 25th percentile and the 75th percentile. An example is depicted in Figure 3, below. For this example, the minimum is 3.4, the 25th percentile is 4.7, the median is 5.7, the 75th percentile is 8.1 and the maximum is 12.

Figure 3: A box-and-whiskers diagram

3.4 4.7 5.7 8.1 12

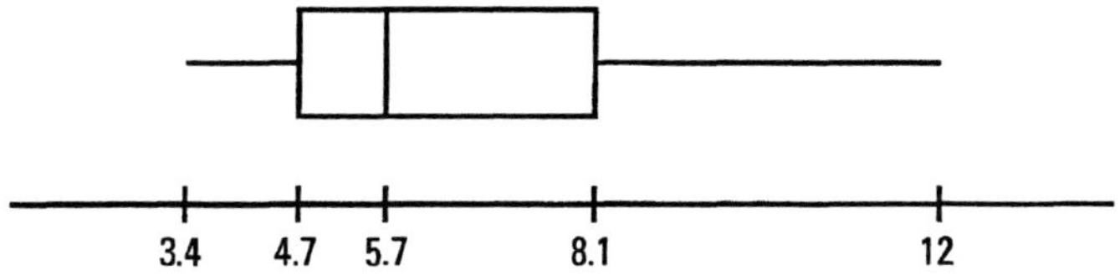

Depicting Paired Data

In **paired data** there is a series of observations, each with two values: say (x_1, y_1), (x_2, y_2), …, (x_n, y_n). For example, if a chemical engineer measures the arsenic levels in a stream at various distances from a factory, she will obtain a set of paired data (i.e. distance, arsenic level). This data can be represented by a **scattergram** on x-y axes, in which there is one plot for each data point (see Figure 4, below). Such paired data often results from experimental research, e.g. if a physicist suspends a spring from the roof, attaches different weights to it and records the stretch for each weight.

Figure 4: A scattergram

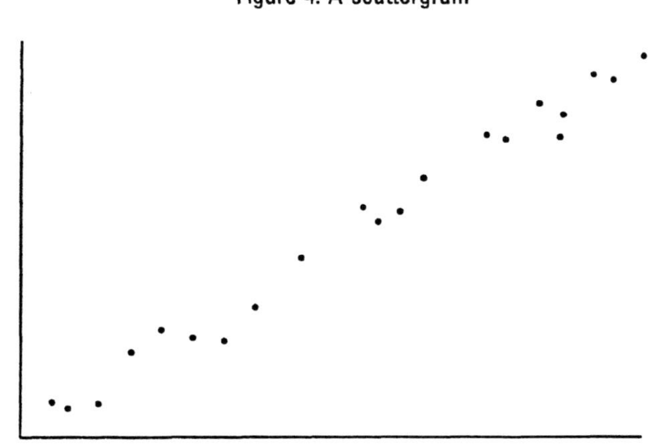

Based on the data, the researcher might propose a curve that 'fits' the data. The data depicted in the example of a scattergram suggests a straight-line fit. We discuss this type of problem next.

8.3 REGRESSION

Suppose a meteorologist accumulates data on temperatures at different altitudes. He would like to know whether there is a mathematical relationship between the two quantities (altitude and temperature). If so, what is this relationship; how strong is this relationship; and can he use the relationship calculated from the data for other temperatures?

Typically, he would start with a scattergram, and examine it for any pattern. The simplest case would be whether there is a straight-line relationship and what the straight line involved is. The process he would use to find the best estimate of a straight-line fit for data is known as **linear regression.** We deal with the question of how good the fit is on the first page of Chapter 11, under the heading **A Test for Linear Correlation.**

In regression, there is a hypothesised function, $y = f(x)$, that is supposed to give the relationship between x and y. The function $f(x)$ starts with some undetermined parameters: in the case of looking for the best line fit, the function is $f(x) = A + Bx$ with parameters A and B. (Remember that B is the slope of the line and A the y-intercept.) The task is to find the best values of the parameters.

In linear regression, the best values of the parameters are given by the following rather intimidating formulas:

$$B = \frac{n(\sum x_i y_i) - (\sum x_i)(\sum y_i)}{n(\sum x_i^2) - (\sum x_i)^2} \text{ and } A = \frac{(\sum y_i) - B(\sum x_i)}{n}$$

The key is to calculate the value of x_i^2 and $x_i y_i$ for each pair (x_i, y_i) of the data, and then calculate the sums. Fortunately, many calculators have a statistical mode for performing such a calculation.

Example: A chemical engineer examined the arsenic levels in a stream as a function of the distance downstream from a factory.

x (distance in km)	2	4	6	8	10	12	14
y (arsenic in mg/kl)	24.5	18.7	16.3	12.0	9.3	6.2	2.5

A scattergram for these data is given in Figure 5, on the next page. This suggests a negative-slope straight-line fit. The results of the regression calculations are laid out in Table 2.

Figure 5: Scattergram for the arsenic example

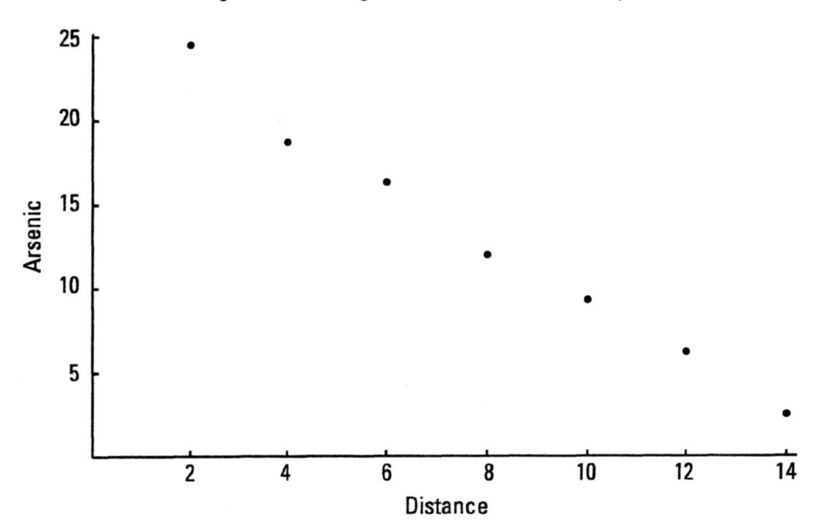

Table 2: Results for the arsenic example

x_i	y_i	x_i^2	x_iy_i
2	24.5	4	49.0
4	18.7	16	74.8
6	16.3	36	97.8
8	12.0	64	96.0
10	9.3	100	93.0
12	6.2	144	74.4
14	2.5	196	35.0
56	89.5	560	520.0

Calculations give $n = 7$, $\sum x_i = 56$, $\sum y_i = 89.5$, $\sum x_iy_i = 520.0$ and $\sum x_i^2 = 560$. The formulas for linear regression give

$$B = \frac{7 \times 520 - 56 \times 89.5}{7 \times 560 - 56^2} = -1.75 \text{ and}$$

$$A = \frac{89.5 - (-1.75) \times 56}{7} = 26.79$$

This means that the best straight-line fit is $y = 26.79 - 1.75x$. Figure 6, below, shows this fit.

Figure 6: Line fit on a scattergram

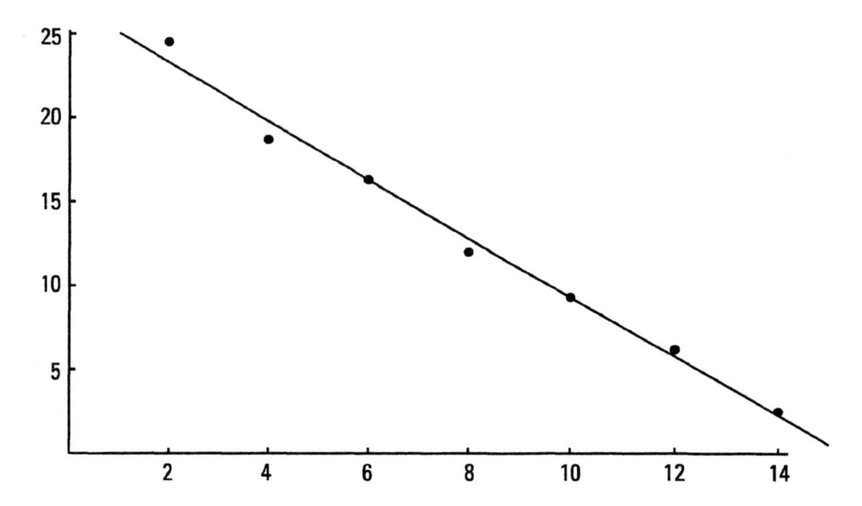

While linear relationships are the most common, there are many other possible relationships. For example, the data in the scattergram in Figure 7, below, suggests a parabolic fit. Regression can be used to find the best fit, but the actual formulas are beyond the scope of this book.

Figure 7: Another scattergram

The process of regression is guaranteed to give a fit. For example, you can fit a line to the data in Figure 7, but this is clearly inappropriate. The best fit is not necessarily a good fit. We will discuss testing whether a fit does in fact reveal a pattern in the data in Chapter 11.

Discussion Questions and Exercises

1. How do we summarise data? Why do we do so?

2. For each of the measures defined in the text, find (a) a situation where the measure is a good summary of the data and (b) one where it is a bad summary.

3. Find some examples of data depiction in newspapers and scientific magazines. Are the images informative or misleading?

4. A geographer measures the relationship between the population sizes of various cities and the number of cinemas in them. The data is:

population sizes (in ten thousands)	1	5	22	23	40	67
cinemas	1	1	10	10	17	28

   a) Plot the data on a scattergram.
   b) Find the best straight-line fit.
   c) Use the line to estimate the number of cinemas in a city of 500 000 inhabitants.

5. A bacteriologist counts the number of yeast cells in a test-tube at various time intervals, with the following results:

yeast	25	60	140	320	700	1 605	3 781	7 017
time	1	2	3	4	5	6	7	8

   a) Plot the data on a scattergram.
   b) Describe in words a curve that would fit the data.
   c) (For the mathematically advanced) Find a fit of the form $y = Ae^{Bx}$. (Use the fact that if $y = Ae^{Bx}$ then $\ln y = \ln A + Bx$, and then use linear regression.)

Chapter 9

Normal Distribution and Estimation

The concept of **probability** is the foundation of statistical tests and processes. We present a brief introduction to probability here. We then introduce the normal distribution, and explain the process of estimation.

9.1 PROBABILITY

The **probability** of an event is the proportion of the time the event can be expected to occur in the long run. For a simple example, consider tossing a coin. If you repeat this 1 000 times, and heads comes up 300 times, then it appears that the probability of heads is $\frac{3}{10}$. (Could a coin act this way? Think about it.)

The probability of an event can also be thought of as the likelihood or chance of it occurring. One classic example is rolling a die. If the die is fair, then there is an equal chance that any of the six sides comes up. So the probability of a fair die coming up with number 5 is 1 out of 6, or, in symbols:

$$\Pr(D = 5) = \tfrac{1}{6}$$

where D stands for the value on the die.

We need some definitions for this process. The rolling of the die is an **experiment**. (In statistics, an experiment is any action where the answer is not predetermined.) The experiment has a number of **outcomes**, and associated with each outcome is a probability. For a repeatable experiment, the probability of a specific outcome amounts to the proportion of the time the outcome is likely to occur. Proportions always lie between 0 and 1, so that if something occurs 40% of the time, then its probability is 0.4. A probability of 0 means that the event never occurs, while a probability of 1 means that it always occurs.

A numerical value resulting from the experiment is known as a **random variable**. A **discrete random variable** takes on only discrete values and often results from counting something; a **continuous random variable** may take on a continuous range of values and often results from measuring something. The quantity D, above, is a discrete random variable. For example, a geologist measures the masses of gold nuggets. This is a continuous random variable; a *random* variable as it is the unknown value resulting from an experiment, and *continuous* as it can have any real number as its outcome.

If you roll a die 600 times, it is very, very unlikely that you will get each number exactly 100 times. However, if some numbers seem to come up a *lot* more than others, then you would suspect that the die was loaded (i.e. not fair). A simulation we ran produced the following frequencies of the numbers from 1 to 6: 86, 112, 122, 95, 98, 87. What do you think about the die?

The question of when to conclude that a die is loaded is precisely the type of question that statistics is designed for. And the short answer is: *if the probability of a result as extreme is sufficiently small, then you may conclude that the die is loaded.*

9.2 PROBABILITY DISTRIBUTIONS

There can be an experiment with just two outcomes, such as tossing a coin. These outcomes are often referred to as **success** and **failure**, and the experiment as a **trial**. To obtain useful data, the researcher repeats the trial several times and counts the number of successes.

For example, suppose we have a trial with a 60% chance of success. If we perform it 9 times and get 5 successes, how likely is that? The following formula gives the answer to such questions:

$$\Pr(S = k) = \frac{n!}{k!\ (n - k)!} p^k(1 - p)^{n - k}$$

where

$g! = g \times (g - 1) \times (g - 2) \times \ldots \times 2 \times 1$, for g nonzero, and 1 for g zero
S is the random variable counting the successes
n is the number of trials
p is the probability of success in a single trial
k is the desired number of successes

In the example of the trial with a 60% chance of success, we need the case $n = 9$, $p = 0.6$ and $k = 5$.

The calculation says $126 \times 0.6^5 \times 0.4^4 = 25.1\%$.

The random variable S is known as a **binomial random variable**. The **probability distribution** of a random variable depicts the probability of each outcome for the variable. Figure 8, below, shows the probability distribution for the binomial random variable with $n = 14$ and $p = \frac{1}{2}$.

Figure 8: A binomial distribution

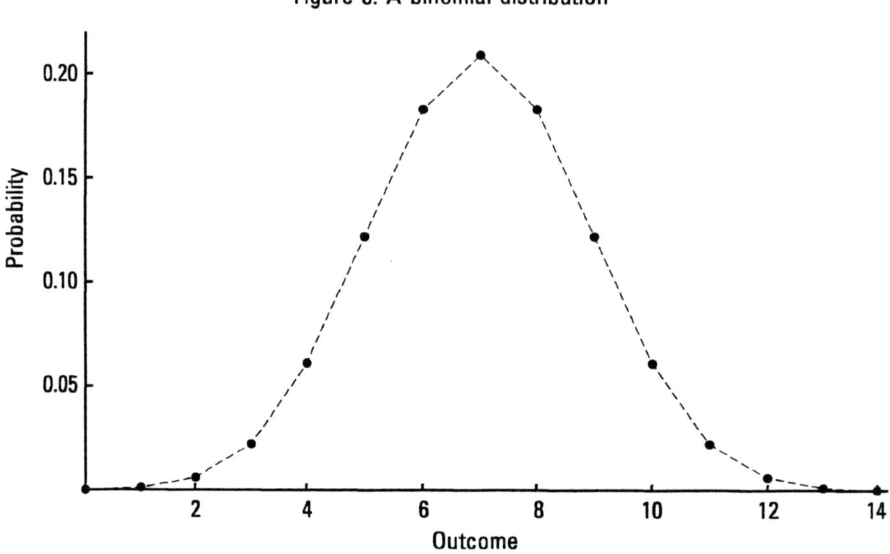

We have made one assumption that we would like to stress: *that the success or failure of one trial does not affect the (probability of) success or failure of another trial.* To be so, statisticians would say the trials must be **independent** events. If the trials are **dependent**, i.e. not independent, then the formula given above is not valid. If I toss one coin and then another coin, the results are independent. If I measure the height and mass of one child, the results are dependent.

There are other useful probability distributions, including the normal, exponential, geometric and Poisson distributions. Of these, the normal distribution is the most important.

9.3 THE NORMAL DISTRIBUTION

The most common probability distribution for a continuous random variable is the **normal distribution.** Figure 9, on the next page, shows the smooth, bell-shaped curve of the normal distribution.

A normal distribution has two parameters: its mean and its standard deviation. The distribution with $\mu = 0$ and $\sigma = 1$ is the standard normal distribution, and the associated random variable is often denoted by z. Many naturally occurring things have a normal distribution, including heights of people, running speeds of ostriches and the birth mass of babies.

Figure 9: The normal distribution

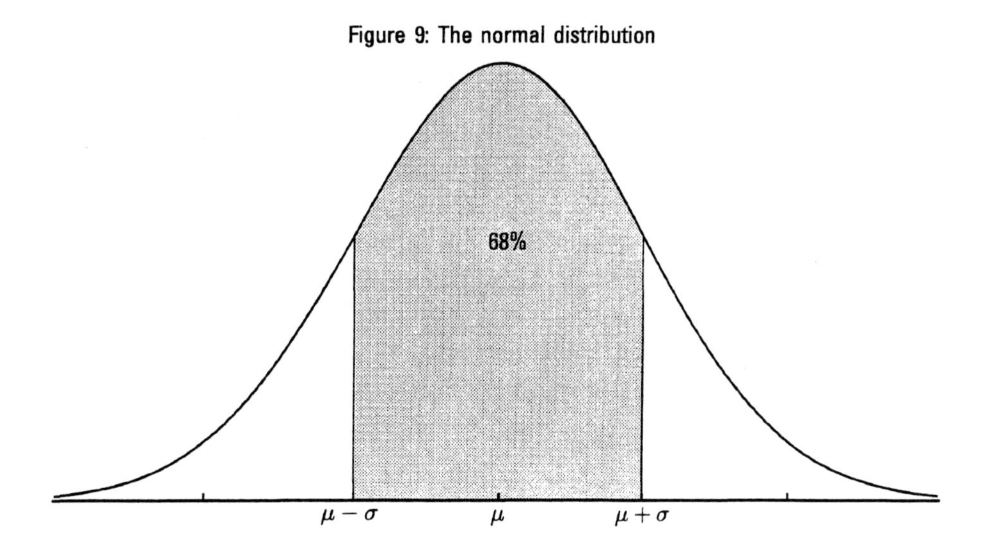

Using Normal Tables

A table of the standard normal distribution is given in Appendix B. This gives the proportion of the population that is less than or equal to z for various values of z.

For example, suppose that the heights of South African men had a mean of 1.77 m and a standard deviation of 4 cm, and one wanted to know what proportion is less than or equal to 1.87 m tall. The method comprises two steps:

1. Calculate the z-value by the formula:

$$z = \frac{x - \mu}{\sigma}$$

2. Look up the proportion in the table in Appendix B.

For this example, $z = \frac{(187 - 177)}{4} = 2.5$. Now consult Appendix B. The proportion is 0.994.

If you need to find what proportion is greater than z, simply use 1 minus the proportion less than z. For example, the proportion of men that are more than 1.87 m tall is $1 - 0.994 = 0.006$ or 0.6%.

9.4 STATISTICAL ESTIMATION

A fundamental problem of statistics is the estimation of measures of populations such as the population mean and standard deviation. A **point estimate** is a single-value estimate of the population measure. A **confidence interval** gives a range of values in which the measure probably lies. Typically the confidence interval is such that there is either a 95% or 99% chance that the actual measure lies in the interval.

The value α (the Greek letter alpha) denotes the probability of error (i.e. the measure lying outside the interval). So the probability of being correct is $1 - \alpha$. For example, for a 95% interval $\alpha = 0.05$ (5%) and for a 99% interval $\alpha = 0.01$ (1%). Confidence intervals are (usually) constructed such that the probability of error is shared equally between the two sides: the probability that the actual measure is above the interval is $\frac{\alpha}{2}$ and the probability that it is below the interval is $\frac{\alpha}{2}$.

In this book, we discuss the problem of estimating the population mean. The **sample mean** is denoted by $\bar{x}$ and is defined as the average of the n sample values:

$$\bar{x} = \frac{1}{n}\sum_{i=1}^{n} x_i$$

The sample mean is a point estimate of the population mean μ.

To determine a confidence interval for the population mean, we will need, in addition to the sample mean, the **sample standard deviation.** The sample standard deviation s is defined by:

$$s = \sqrt{\frac{\sum_{i=1}^{n}(x_i - \bar{x})^2}{n - 1}}$$

This is similar to the formula for the population standard deviation σ except that there is the value $n - 1$ in the denominator rather than n. (There is a deep statistical reason for this difference, which we do not explore here.) There is an alternative formula that is easier for calculations:

$$s = \sqrt{\frac{\sum x_i^2 - n \times \bar{x}^2}{n - 1}}$$

Example: For the sample data 8, 12, 10, 16, 7, 13
the sample mean is 11
the sample standard deviation is:

$$\sqrt{\frac{782 - 6 \times 112}{5}} = \sqrt{\frac{56}{5}} = 3.35$$

In this section, we discuss two common situations where confidence intervals for the mean can be provided.

The Large-sample Method for Estimating the Mean

The large-sample method can be reliably applied if there are at least 30 data values. Given some choice of α, a $1 - \alpha$ confidence interval for μ is given by:

$$\bar{x} - z \times \frac{s}{\sqrt{n}} < \mu < \bar{x} + z \times \frac{s}{\sqrt{n}}$$

In this expression, the value z is obtained from the table in Appendix C by looking up the entry in the **two-tailed** column corresponding to the chosen value of the error α. (The two-tailed values are always used for confidence intervals.)

For example, suppose we wanted to be 95% sure that the value of μ lay within the interval. Then we would choose α to be 5% (i.e. 0.05), and obtain the value 1.96 for z in the column corresponding to 95% and two-tailed. (Remember that we divide the chance of error equally on both sides or **tails**, so that there is a 2.5% chance of the actual value of μ being smaller than the calculated lower bound, and a 2.5% chance of the actual value of μ being larger than the calculated upper bound.)

Example: A biologist measures the salinity of the leaves of 60 white mangrove trees in an estuary. She wants to estimate the average salinity with a 99% confidence interval.

Procedure: She calculates the sample mean and sample standard deviation. Say she obtains $\bar{x} = 5.39$ and $s = 2.04$. She looks up the critical value for 99%, two-tailed in Appendix C. The value she finds is 2.58. So a 99% confidence interval for the salinity is:

$$[5.39 - 2.58 \times \frac{2.04}{\sqrt{60}}, 5.39 + 2.58 \times \frac{2.04}{\sqrt{60}}] = [4.71, 6.07]$$

The Small-sample Method

You can estimate the population mean from a small sample if you know that the underlying population has a normal distribution, or you have good reason to believe this. In this case, the sample mean $\bar{x}$ is related to Student's t distribution (so called because the discoverer, Gosset, published the work under the pseudonym 'Student'). The process of estimation is the same as in the large-sample method, except that you look up values in the t-table given in Appendix D, rather than in the z-table.

The t distribution has a bell-shaped curve. It has one parameter, df, which is known as its **degrees of freedom**. If df is small, the curve is a bit more peaked than the normal distribution, but if df is large, the two curves are indistinguishable.

A $1 - \alpha$ confidence interval (the value α denotes the probability of error) is given by:

$$\bar{x} - t \times \frac{s}{\sqrt{n}} < \mu < \bar{x} + t \times \frac{s}{\sqrt{n}}$$

The value t is found in the t-table on the row for $n - 1$ degrees of freedom in the appropriate column for the α-value required (again, the two-tailed values are used).

Example revisited: In the previous example, we used the large-sample method to determine a 99% confidence interval for mangrove salinity. Say our biologist could only obtain 20 leaves, and again obtained a sample mean of 5.39, but a sample standard deviation of 1.84. Since she believes that the salinity has a normal distribution, she uses the small-sample method. Degrees of freedom $df = 20 - 1 = 19$. $\alpha = 0.01$ (i.e. there is a 1% chance of error). The value in the table is 2.861. So the confidence interval is:

$$\left[5.39 - 2.861 \times \frac{1.84}{\sqrt{20}}, 5.39 + 2.861 \times \frac{1.84}{\sqrt{20}}\right] = [4.21, 6.57]$$

This example shows that a confidence interval can be narrowed by taking n larger (think about why). This means that the larger the sample, the better the estimate.

Discussion Questions and Exercises

1. If you roll two fair dice, what is the probability of getting double sixes? Any double? An odd number for the total?

2. From the population of the digits 0 through 9, take a random sample of three digits. Calculate μ, σ, $\bar{x}$ and s.

3. Say the size of king protea flowers is normally distributed with mean 127 mm and standard deviation 13 mm. What proportion is more than 140 mm?

4. Find a 95% confidence interval for the population mean from the sample data
   7.2, 9.3, 10.2, 11.4, 14.8, 16, 10.3, 11.4, 12.3, 9.9, 8,
   stating any assumptions you make.

5. Find a 99% confidence interval for the population mean if the sample size is 50, the sample mean is 43.41 and the sample standard deviation is 2.61.

Chapter 10

Testing Hypotheses

A fundamental principle in the scientific method is the formulation of hypotheses. Once a researcher has formulated a hypothesis and accumulated the data, he analyses the data and then accepts or rejects the hypothesis. In this chapter, we describe this process, from the formulation of the hypothesis to the testing of the data.

The purpose of a hypothesis is to predict a relationship between variables that can be tested. Hypotheses direct a researcher's work by indicating what procedures should be followed. This means that hypotheses may be reformulated *before* empirical studies start, but not *afterwards*.

10.1 HYPOTHESES, ERRORS AND TAILS

Hypotheses

Any statistical test revolves around the choice between two hypotheses. These are labelled H_0 and H_1. H_0 is often called the **null hypothesis**.

We asked in a previous chapter how you would decide if a coin were fair. In this case, the null hypothesis, H_0, would be that the coin is fair. The alternative, H_1, would be that it is biased.

Errors

Consider the following example: A biotechnology firm develops a new drug against tuberculosis. To test the drug, they administer the drug to some patients and a placebo to others. They then compare the results to determine whether the drug is effective or not. Suppose H_0 is that the drug has no effect, and H_1 that the drug is effective.

There are two possible ways the answer could be wrong. One possibility is that the research staff doing the test conclude that the drug is effective, when in fact it has no effect. The other possibility is that they conclude that the drug has no effect, when in fact it does. These are known as **Type I** and **Type II** errors respectively.

Ideally, one would like neither error to occur, but this is impossible. The smaller the risk of one type of error, the greater the risk of the other type. If a researcher is not prepared to accept any risk of a Type I error, then she must accept a high risk of a Type II error, and vice versa. (Think about why this should be so.)

In a hypothesis test, the researcher takes as H_0 the situation that he/she doesn't mind being accepted as true when it is in fact false, and takes an alternative as H_1. The *benefit of the doubt goes to the hypothesis H_0*. In other words, the researcher focuses on the probability of a Type I error. This probability is denoted by α. The probability of a Type II error is denoted by β (beta). This process is laid out in Table 3, below.

Table 3: Types of errors

	H_0 true	H_1 true
H_0 accepted	Okay	Type II error
H_1 accepted	Type I error	Okay

Hypotheses and Tails

An agricultural researcher wishes to test a new fertiliser, to see if it increases maize yield. There are four possible hypotheses:

H_0: The fertiliser does not affect maize yield.
H_{1a}: The fertiliser does affect maize yield.
H_{1b}: The fertiliser increases maize yield.
H_{1c}: The fertiliser decreases maize yield.

Hypothesis H_{1a} allows for either an increase in yield or a decrease in yield, i.e. it is a combination of hypotheses H_{1b} and H_{1c}. Since there are two ways in which hypothesis H_{1a} can be true, it is termed a **two-tailed test**. Hypotheses H_{1b} and H_{1c}, on the other hand, only test for a difference in one direction (i.e. at one extreme only), and are termed **one-tailed tests**. H_{1b} is an example of an **upper-tail test**, whereas H_{1c} is an example of a **lower-tail test**. Whenever hypothesis H_1 uses a relative term (e.g. heavier, less than), it is a one-tailed test. Whenever H_1 states a difference *without* specifying the direction of the difference (e.g. unequal, affects), then the test is two-tailed.

When the test is one-tailed, the null hypothesis must be adjusted accordingly. In our example above, if H_{1b} is used, then H_0 would be that the fertiliser does *not increase* the maize yield. Similarly, if H_{1c} is used, then H_0 would be that the fertiliser does *not decrease* the maize yield. In all cases, H_0 is the *opposite* of H_1, i.e. any situation not covered by H_1 is covered by H_0. Figures 10a, 10b and 10c, below, show this diagrammatically.

Figure 10a: A two-tailed test

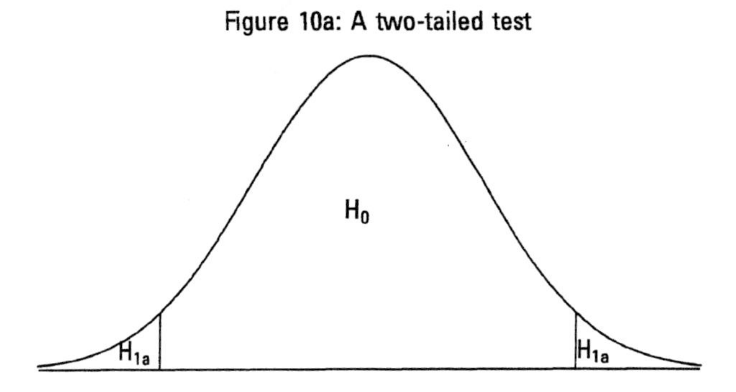

Figure 10b: An upper-tail test

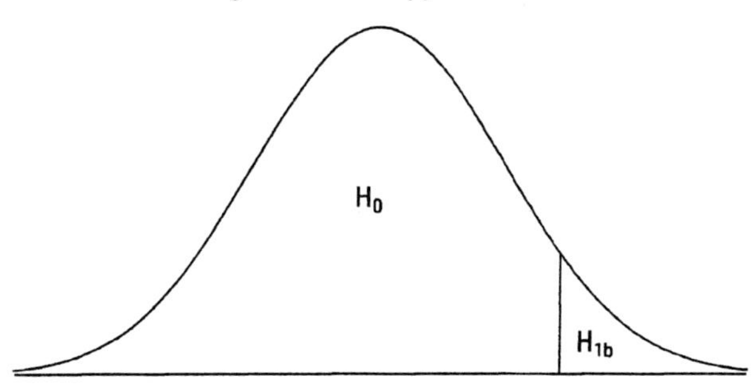

Figure 10c: A lower-tail test

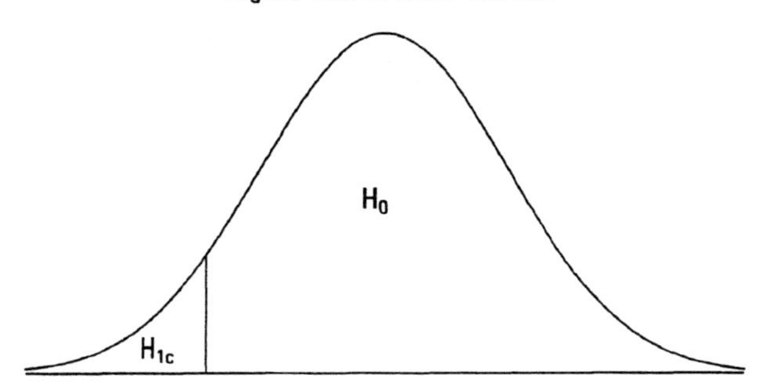

Level of Significance

A hypothesis test is based on the probability of sample data being as extreme as the data encountered, assuming that H_0 is true. This is α, the probability of Type I error. The researcher must choose a level of significance, i.e. an upper limit for α. Common levels are 5% and 1%. For a test at the 5% level of significance, there is at most a 5% chance of Type I error. In reporting the results of a hypothesis test, the researcher must state the level of significance.

10.2 THE STEPS IN A HYPOTHESIS TEST

In every statistical test, the procedure is as follows:

1. Identify which test is appropriate.
2. Choose a level of significance α.
3. Formulate H_0 and H_1.
4. Determine whether the test is one-tailed or two-tailed. If it is one-tailed, determine whether it is an upper- or a lower-tail test.
5. Calculate the test statistic.
6. Based on the chosen level for α, compare the test statistic with a value from a table (the **critical value**).
7. Conclude by either accepting or rejecting H_1.

In particular, suppose we have a test statistic u and a table value v. Then H_1 is accepted:

a) in a two-tailed test, if $u > v$ or $u < -v$;
b) in a one-tailed, upper-tail test, if $u > v$; and
c) in a one-tailed, lower-tail test, if $u < -v$.

If H_1 is accepted, then H_0 must be rejected. However, since tests are structured so that the benefit of the doubt goes to H_0, the converse is not true, i.e. the fact that one cannot be 95% (say) sure of H_1 does *not* mean that one is 95% sure of H_0 (think about it). So if H_1 is rejected, we simply state that H_0 is *not* rejected.

10.3 TESTS OF THE MEAN OF ONE SAMPLE

A researcher takes a sample and has a value in mind for the population mean μ. Then the question is, does the sample $\bar{x}$ contradict this value significantly? This is similar to the estimation of the mean from the sample mean described in the previous chapter.

We will describe two versions:

- the large-sample (z) test; and
- the small-sample (t) test.

The large-sample test can be used if the sample size is greater than 30, while the small-sample test can be used if the sample comes from a normal distribution (regardless of sample size).

In the test, the H_1 hypothesis is that the population mean is either different from (two-tailed), greater than (one-tailed, upper tail) or less than (one-tailed, lower tail) a particular value. H_0 is the opposite of this, i.e.:

$H_0 : \mu = c$, $\quad H_1 : \mu \neq c$;
$H_0 : \mu \leq c$, $\quad H_1 : \mu > c$; or
$H_0 : \mu \geq c$, $\quad H_1 : \mu < c$;

The sample statistics are denoted by n, $\bar{x}$ and s. The large-sample test uses the following test statistic:

$$z = \frac{\bar{x} - \mu}{s}\sqrt{n}$$

The test statistic calculated is compared to a value from the z-table. The small-sample test uses the following test statistic:

$$t = \frac{\bar{x} - \mu}{s}\sqrt{n}$$

The test statistic calculated is compared to a value from the t-table with $df = n - 1$.

Example 1: A climatologist measures the freezing points of water taken from 42 different lakes. He wants to test whether the average freezing point is 0 degrees Celsius, and be 95% sure of his conclusion. The sample statistics are $\bar{x} = -0.49$ and $s = 1.23$.

Procedure:
1. The test is a large-sample test.
2. The significance level is 0.05.
3. H_0: the population mean is 0.
   H_1: the population mean is not 0.
4. This is a two-tailed test.
5. The test statistic is:

$$z = \frac{-0.49 - 0}{1.23}\sqrt{42} = -2.58$$

6. The table value for the 5% level of significance is 1.96.
7. Accept H_1, as $-2.58 < -1.96$. There is sufficient evidence to conclude that the population mean is not 0.

Example 2: It is known that the I.Q. of humans has a normal distribution with mean 100. Researchers believe that the I.Q.s of rugby players are higher. They select 20 members of rugby teams using cluster sampling (each team forming a cluster), and test them for I.Q. The sample mean is 102.7 and the sample standard deviation 14.8. Are the I.Q.s of rugby players higher?

Procedure: The test is the small-sample t-test. H_0 is that rugby players have normal or below normal I.Q.s, while H_1 is that rugby players have higher than normal I.Q.s. This is a one-tailed, upper-tail test. The calculated test statistic is $t = 0.816$ and the degrees of freedom $df = 19$. The value in the table is 1.73 for the 5% level of significance. As $0.816 < 1.73$, at the 5% level of significance the researchers cannot conclude that rugby players have higher I.Q.s.

Estimation and Hypothesis Testing

These hypothesis tests of the population mean are linked to the estimation of population mean discussed in Chapter 9, in the section headed **Statistical Estimation.** For example, in a two-sided test, H_0 is rejected if, and only if, $\bar{x}$ is outside the confidence interval.

10.4 A TEST FOR EQUIVALENCE OF RELATED SAMPLES

Related sample pairs can be formed in two ways. One way is where two sets of measurements are compared (e.g. the results of before-and-after tests on the masses of mice). The other is where the data is gathered from measurements of matched samples (see **Matching** in Chapter 5).

To perform the test on pairs (a_i, b_i), you calculate the difference data $d_i = a_i - b_i$. The difference data is itself a sample. For a two-tailed test, the null hypothesis H_0 is that the two population means are equal. This is the same as testing whether the population mean μ_D of the difference data is zero, i.e. H_0 is that $\mu_D = 0$. Hypothesis H_1 is that μ_D is non-zero. We use the difference data for a t-test. The sample statistics for the difference data are denoted n, $\bar{x}_d$ and s_d. Note that for matched data, n denotes the number of data *pairs*.

The t-test for equivalence of related samples uses the following test statistic:

$$t = \frac{\bar{x}_d}{s_d}\sqrt{n}$$

Degrees of freedom: $df = n - 1$.

Example: An educator proposes that using multimedia would improve the teaching of calculus to first-year students. So she picks a sample group of 20 students at random. She matches students in terms of matric mathematics symbols into 10 pairs, with one member of each pair being placed in the experimental group and the other in the control group. The measurements she uses as data are the final calculus exam marks of the students.

Procedure: The test is the t-test for equivalence of related samples. The educator decided to do the test at both the 1% and 5% levels of significance. Hypothesis H_0 is that the use of multimedia has no effect on or worsens the calculus results. Hypothesis H_1 is that the use of multimedia improves the calculus results. The test is one-tailed, upper tail. The measured data is tabulated in Table 4, below.

Table 4: Results for the calculus example

Pair	Marks group: experiment	Marks group: control	Difference	d_i^2
a	18	16	2	4
b	16	15	1	1
c	14	15	−1	1
d	16	16	0	0
e	17	10	7	49
f	14	10	4	16
g	12	15	−3	9
h	13	8	5	25
i	11	11	0	0
j	9	5	4	16
Totals			19	121

Calculations: $\bar{x}_D = 1.9$ and $s_D = 3.07$, so that the test statistic is $t = 1.9 \frac{\sqrt{10}}{3.07} = 1.96$. The number of degrees of freedom is $df = 9$, so the critical values are 1.83 and 2.82. The educator can therefore assume an improvement at the 5% level of significance but not at the 1% level of significance (i.e. she can be 95% certain that H_1 is true, but not 99% certain).

Notes:

1. You must check the necessary assumptions for hypothesis tests. If you do not know them to be true beforehand, you may have to carry out further statistics tests.
2. It is sometimes advisable to estimate β, the chance of a Type II error.

Discussion Questions and Exercises

1. Explain the meaning of the following terms: hypothesis, null hypothesis, tail, level of significance, hypothesis test, test statistic, critical value.

2. In drug testing, the null hypothesis is normally that the drug has no effect, and the alternative is that the drug is effective.
   a) What are Type I and Type II errors in these circumstances?
   b) Which is preferable?
   c) What about a disease such as HIV/Aids, which is rampant and for which no cure has been found yet? Should one deny people a drug just because one is not totally convinced that it is effective? Discuss.

3. The sample data of Question 4 in the **Discussion questions and exercises** in Chapter 9 is believed to come from a population with mean 12.8. Test the hypothesis that:
   a) this is not true; and
   b) the actual mean is smaller than 12.8.

4. If we always use a 0.05 level of significance, does this mean that on average one out of 20 conclusions will be wrong?

5. A quantity surveyor calculates the amount of material needed for a project as 60 units. For a sample of 40 projects he obtains a mean of 65.32 units and a standard deviation of 3.17 units. Test to see whether the sample data conforms with his calculations.

6. A student makes a series of measurements of the same compound on two scales in milligrams and obtains the following results:

   Scale 1: 473 321 555 678 299 407
   Scale 2: 472 320 556 682 307 415

   a) Find a 95% confidence interval for the average difference between the two scales.
   b) Test the belief that Scale 2 gives higher readings than Scale 1.
   c) What does this say, if anything, about the validity and reliability of the two scales?

Chapter 11

More Hypothesis Testing

In this chapter, we describe some frequently used tests. First we describe a test for linear correlation, and then introduce the concept of partial correlation. Then we describe two more tests: the chi-square test for patterns in frequency data and the test for the equality of means for independent samples.

11.1 A TEST FOR LINEAR CORRELATION

In the section entitled **Regression** in Chapter 8, we described how to find the best line fit for paired data. Determining whether there is in fact a linear relationship requires another hypothesis test. Pearson's product-moment **coefficient of linear correlation** is calculated by the following formula:

$$r = \frac{n\sum x_i y_i - (\sum x_i)(\sum y_i)}{\sqrt{n\sum x_i^2 - (\sum x_i)^2}\sqrt{n\sum y_i^2 - (\sum y_i)^2}}$$

(Wow!) This parameter lies between -1 and 1. A value of 1 indicates a perfect linear dependence with a positive slope. (An increase in the value of variable x is associated with a proportionate *increase* in the value of variable y.) A value of -1 indicates a perfect linear dependence with a negative slope. (An increase in the value of variable x is associated with a proportionate *decrease* in the value of variable y.) A value of 0 or thereabouts says very little.

The hypothesis test H_1 can be that either:

a) there is a linear correlation (two-tailed); or
b) there is a positive-slope correlation (one-tailed, upper tail); or
c) there is a negative-slope correlation (one-tailed, lower tail).

The hypothesis H_0 is, as usual, the opposite of H_1. The test statistic is the Pearson coefficient of linear correlation r. The test statistic is compared with the critical values obtained from the table in Appendix E, with $n - 2$ degrees of freedom (where n is the number of data pairs), and value desired of α.

Example: In the section entitled **Regression** in Chapter 8 we considered a chemical engineer who obtained the measurements set out below for arsenic levels at different distances from a factory. The engineer wishes to test whether the arsenic distances decrease linearly the further one is from the factory.

x (distance in km)	2	4	6	8	10	12	14
y (arsenic in mg/kl)	24.5	18.7	16.3	12.0	9.3	6.2	2.5

Procedure: This is a one-tailed, lower-tail test with H_0 that arsenic levels do not decrease linearly with distance from factory, and H_1 that arsenic levels do decrease linearly with distance from the factory.

Calculations give $n = 7$, $\sum x_i = 56$, $\sum y_i = 89.5$, $\sum x_i y_i = 520.0$, $\sum x_i^2 = 560$ and $\sum y_i^2 = 1490.81$. Hence:

$$r = \frac{7 \times 520 - 56 \times 89.5}{\sqrt{7 \times 560 - 56^2} \times \sqrt{7 \times 1\,490.81 - 89.5^2}} = -0.995$$

The $df = 7 - 2 = 5$. Table values are 0.669 (5% level) and 0.833 (1% level). So the engineer can accept H_1 at the 1% level (i.e. he can be 99% certain that H_1 is true).

11.2 PARTIAL CORRELATION

It is important to note that the existence of high linear correlation between two variables does not necessarily imply a cause-and-effect relationship between the two variables. For example, it is likely that ownership of motor vehicles and ownership of television sets have a high correlation. This does not mean that owning a car *causes* someone to own a television set. Some other factor could be at work, e.g. wealth.

Partial correlation tries to remove the effect of the third variable and thereby find the 'true' relationship between the first and second variables. The formula for partial correlation is:

$$r_{12.3} = \frac{r_{12} - r_{13}r_{23}}{\sqrt{1 - r_{13}^2}\sqrt{1 - r_{23}^2}}$$

where:

- $r_{12.3}$ is the partial correlation between variables 1 and 2 with the effect of variable 3 removed;
- r_{12} is the correlation between variables 1 and 2;
- r_{13} is the correlation between variables 1 and 3;
- r_{23} is the correlation between variables 2 and 3;

and correlation is measured by the Pearson coefficient of linear correlation (see the previous section).

To continue our example, say a researcher found that owning TVs (variable 1) had a correlation of 0.7 with owning cars (variable 2). She also found that the correlation of TV ownership with wealth (variable 3, which the researcher defined as the possession of assets worth over

R50 000) was 0.8, and the correlation of car ownership with wealth was 0.9. The formula gives:

$$r_{12.3} = \frac{0.7 - 0.8 \times 0.9}{\sqrt{1 - 0.8^2}\sqrt{1 - 0.9^2}} = -0.08$$

In other words, the researcher finds almost no correlation at all (−0.08 is a tiny negative correlation) between TV ownership and car ownership once the effect of wealth has been removed.

11.3 THE CHI-SQUARE TEST

In this section we describe the **chi-square test** for dependence of two qualitative variables. For example, the colour of a particular chemical solution can be red, orange, purple or blue and its acidity can be categorised as high, medium or low. We wish to know if colour and acidity are related.

Say the first qualitative variable divides the entire population up into R classes and the second divides the entire population up into C classes. In our example above, $R = 4$ and $C = 3$. To apply the chi-square test, the researcher takes a sample of the population and categorises each item according to both variables. The sample items are divided into R classes according to the first variable and into C classes according to the second.

The data is represented in a **contingency table**. Each row corresponds to a different class of the first variable and each column to a different class of the second variable. The entry o_{ij} in row i and column j gives the number of sample items that are classified as class i for the first variable and class j for the second. Table 5 shows the observed frequencies for our example. Totals for each row and column are calculated, as well as the overall total.

Table 5: Observed frequencies

	High	Medium	Low	Row total
Red	15	8	5	28
Orange	12	9	9	30
Purple	25	24	31	80
Blue	6	14	20	40
Column total	58	55	65	178

Next, we construct the **expected contingency table** that would result if the two variables were independent. To calculate the entry e_{ij} in row i and column j of the expected contingency table, we multiply the total in row i by the total in column j and divide the result by the overall total. The expected contingency table for our example is given in Table 6.

Table 6: Expected frequencies

	High	Medium	Low
Red	9.12	8.65	10.22
Orange	9.78	9.27	10.96
Purple	26.07	24.72	29.21
Blue	13.03	12.36	14.61

In the test, the hypothesis H_0 is that the two variables are independent and H_1 is that they are dependent. The test statistic is:

$$\chi^2 = \sum \frac{(o_{ij} - e_{ij})^2}{e_{ij}}$$

where o_{ij} denotes the observed frequency in row i, column j, and e_{ij} the expected frequency in row i, column j, and the summation is over all entries in the contingency table.

For the above data, the contribution to the test statistic χ^2 is laid out in Table 7, below.

Table 7: The contribution to the test statistic

3.785	0.049	2.670
0.506	0.008	0.349
0.044	0.021	0.109
3.796	0.218	1.991

For example, the entry 2.670 is calculated by $\frac{(5 - 10.22)^2}{10.22}$.

We need to compare this with the chi-square tables. The degrees of freedom for a x^2 test are given by $(r - 1)(c - 1)$. In our example above, which is a 4-by-3 table, this is $df = (4 - 1)(3 - 1) = 6$. The concept of a lower tail does not exist for the χ^2 test statistic, as the statistic is always positive. As all the error is then in the upper tail, a two-tailed test becomes an upper-tail test.

The null hypothesis H_0 is that colour and acidity are independent, H_1 is that colour and acidity are dependent, and the test statistic is $\chi^2 = 13.546$ with $df = 2 \times 3 = 6$. So critical values are 12.59 (5%) and 16.81 (1%). We would therefore accept at the 5% level of significance but not at the 1% level of significance.

There are limitations on the use of this test. An important rule of thumb is that every entry in the expected contingency table must be at least 5.

The chi-square test is an example of a **non-parametric test**. Such tests can be used when the data is qualitative or discrete, as they do not assume anything about the underlying distribution of the population. Such tests are especially useful if the data is ordinal rather than cardinal (i.e. the data items are ranked from 1 to n rather than having values showing quantity).

Comparing One Qualitative Variable with a Theory

Researchers can use a version of the chi-square test where they have frequency data and wish to check whether this conforms with a theorised distribution. For example, someone might wish to test whether data comes from a random distribution or not.

There is one qualitative variable. Say this divides the population into M classes. The data gives the observed frequencies o_i, and the theorised distribution gives the expected frequencies e_i. Then the test statistic is given by a similar formula to the one above:

$$\chi^2 = \sum \frac{(o_i - e_i)^2}{e_i}$$

There are $M - 1$ degrees of freedom.

Example: The final episode in the case of the loaded die! Recall that we rolled a (simulated) die 600 times and got results for the numbers from 1 to 6 of 86, 112, 122, 95, 98, 87. Is this die loaded?

Procedure: Hypothesis H_0 is that the die is fair, while hypothesis H_1 is that it is loaded. Expected values are 100 each. The test has 5 degrees of freedom. The test statistic is $\chi^2 = 10.22$ (the calculation is $\frac{(-14)^2}{100} + \frac{12^2}{100} + \frac{22^2}{100} + \frac{(-5)^2}{100} + \frac{(-2)^2}{100} + \frac{(-3)^2}{100)}$). Testing at the 5% level, we find that the table value is 11.07. So we cannot reject the hypothesis that the die is fair.

Tests with One Degree of Freedom

In general, the chi-square test is a test of dependence. However, in the special case where $df = 1$, a researcher can test for a one-tailed hypothesis. One case is a 2-by-2 contingency table. For example, a researcher may be testing a new drug with two categories, i.e. drug and placebo, and with two results, i.e. recover or not recover. He can use a chi-square test to test whether the drug is effective or not. Another case is illustrated in the next example.

Example: An economist wrote a computer program to forecast whether the next day's JSE industrial average would be higher than today's. She ran it for three months. She knows that an increase occurs on average 3 days out of 5. As the program's forecast was right only 66 days out of 90, a cynical colleague suggests that the economist might as well toss a coin that comes up heads 60% of the time. Is he correct?

Procedure: This test is the chi-test for one qualitative variable. H_0 is that $\mu = 0.6$ and H_1 is that $\mu > 0.6$. This is a one-tailed test. The observed frequencies are 66 (correct) and 24 (incorrect). The expected frequencies are $(\frac{3}{5}) \times 90 = 54$ (correct) and $(\frac{2}{5}) \times 90 = 36$ (incorrect). The test statistic is $\chi^2 = \frac{(66-54)^2}{54} + \frac{(24-36)^2}{36} = 6.67$. The value in the table is 2.71 (5% level) and 5.51 (1% level). Therefore, the economist can conclude with 99% confidence that the program is worthwhile.

11.4 TESTS FOR EQUALITY OF MEANS (INDEPENDENT SAMPLES)

Another situation a researcher may encounter is where he has two independent samples from different populations, but wonders whether the means are the same.

We describe two tests here. These are the large-sample (z) test and the small-sample (t) test. The t-test can only be applied if both samples come from normal populations, and the standard deviations of the normal populations are similar. (The equality of standard deviations can be checked by using what is known as the F-test.)

In both tests there are two samples, which we denote by A and B. The null hypothesis H_0 in a two-tailed test is that the two population means (which we denote by μ_A and μ_B) are equal. The sample statistics for A are denoted by n_A, $\bar{x}_A$ and s_A, and for B by n_B, $\bar{x}_B$ and s_B.

The z-test for equality of means (large samples) uses the test statistic:

$$z = \frac{\bar{x}_A - \bar{x}_B}{\sqrt{\frac{s_A^2}{n_a} + \frac{s_B^2}{n_B}}}$$

The t-test for equality of means (normal populations) uses the test statistic:

$$t = \frac{\bar{x}_A - \bar{x}_B}{\sqrt{(n_A - 1)s_A^2 + (n_B - 1)s_B^2}} \sqrt{\frac{n_a n_B(n_A + n_B - 2)}{n_A + n_B}}$$

with $df = n_A + n_B - 2$ degrees of freedom.

A large-sample example: A large software house uses the languages C and Natural for programming. Management wish to compare the development times of the two languages, as they believe that Natural is quicker to use. They know that recently they have completed 42 projects in Natural and 30 in C. The sample statistics in person-months are $\bar{x}_N = 3.3$, $s_N = 1.1$, $\bar{x}_C = 4.0$ and $s_C = 0.8$.

Procedure: The test is the two-sample z-test. H_0 is that Natural is the same or slower than C, and H_1 that Natural is quicker. This is a one-tailed, lower-tail test. The test statistic is $z = -3.13$. Critical values are -1.64 (5%) and -2.33 (1%). As the test statistic is less than both critical values, the software house can conclude with 99% certainty that Natural is quicker to use.

A small-sample example: A zoologist has developed a new nutrient that when taken as a supplement by rats is believed to increase mass by at least 4 g. He tested the nutrient on rats, using an experimental group of 10 rats and a control group of 10 rats. He has good reason to believe that mass gain is normally distributed. In the control group, the gain statistics in grams were $\bar{x}_C = 37.3$ and $s_C = 4.2$. In the experimental group, they were $\bar{x}_E = 44.6$ and $s_E = 4.7$.

Procedure: The test is the two-sample t-test. H_0 is that the nutrient increases mass by 4 g or less, and H_1 that the nutrient increases mass by more than 4 g. This is a one-tailed test (upper tail). The test statistic is $t = 1.66$. The degrees of freedom are $df = 18$. Critical values from the table are 1.73 (5% level) and 2.55 (1% level). Therefore, the zoologist can be 95% certain that the nutrient increases weight by more than 4 g, but not 99% certain.

There is also an extension of these tests to a null hypothesis H_0 in a two-tailed test in the form $\mu_A - \mu_B = C$. The test statistics are the same as those in the above formulas, except that the numerator $\bar{x}_A - \bar{x}_B$ is replaced by $\bar{x}_A - \bar{x}_B - C$.

Discussion Questions and Exercises

1. What is linear correlation? What is negative linear correlation? Is it possible to have a negative linear correlation without a linear correlation? Or a linear correlation without a negative one? Or a negative correlation without a negative linear correlation?

2. Test the data of Question 4 of **Discussion questions and exercises** in Chapter 8 for linear correlation.

3. Pick 10 number pairs at random. Each number in each pair should be a whole number in the range 1 to 10. Is there a linear correlation among the number pairs you have chosen?

4. A drug company finally does the trial on a new treatment for tuberculosis. There are 32 patients who complete the trial. Of the 18 patients on placebo, 8 recover and 10 do not. Of the 15 patients on the drug, 12 recover and 3 do not.
   a) Is there any difference between the effectiveness of the drug and that of the placebo?
   b) What does your result in question a) tell you about the drug?

5. According to Mendel's laws of genetics, the population of plants produced from a certain crop of seedlings should be: red flower green stem, orange flower yellow stem, red flower yellow stem, orange flower green stem in the proportion 9:3:3:1. Researchers sprout a random sample of 100 seeds, and the observed frequencies are 52:19:24:5. Are these results compatible with Mendel's laws?

6. In a case study, a researcher into poverty measures the correlation between income and I.Q. and obtains $r = 0.6$. She also measures the correlation between income and years of schooling, obtaining 0.8, and between years of schooling and I.Q., obtaining 0.55. Use partial correlation to compute the correlation of income and I.Q. without the influence of schooling. What does your result mean?

7. An economist measures the prices of samples of 40 widgets in both Ankara and Bisho in rands. In Ankara he obtains a mean of 14.31 and a standard deviation of 3.12, and in Bisho a mean of 14.64 and a standard deviation of 3.03. Is there a significant difference in the price?

8. Two samples from different normal populations yield the following sample statistics: $n_A = 6$, $\bar{x}_A = 100$, $s_A = 10$, $n_B = 8$, $\bar{x}_B = 80$ and $s_B = 9$. Test for inequality of population means.

Part 4

RESEARCH WRITING

Scientific writing is characterised by conciseness, objectivity and consistency, as well as correct usage of technical terms and established formats. Most importantly, though, scientific writing is a communication – and, as with any communication, it should be clear and unambiguous.

In Chapter 12 we discuss scientific writing in general, in Chapter 13 we explain how to reference other people's work, and in Chapter 14 we outline specific formats for theses and dissertations, research proposals and company reports.

Chapter 12

Scientific Writing

In this chapter, we look at some aspects of scientific writing. We start with a list of useful tips to remember in scientific writing, and then discuss how finished documents should look.

This is not a grammar textbook, and so we do not discuss fundamental aspects of language usage. This in no way implies that grammatical errors are acceptable in scientific writing, but rather demonstrates the expectation that people involved in postgraduate research will already have such skills.

12.1 FOURTEEN TIPS FOR BETTER COMMUNICATION

1. Draw up a Plan

You wouldn't begin a two-week trip to Malawi without some form of plan (itinerary, road maps, traveller's cheques, visas), so why begin a report that could take up to several months (for theses) without one? Map out the order in which you will discuss the points in your presentation, and ensure that your writing follows a logical progression from one point to the next, and from one section to the next. Occasional 'road maps' that summarise the section or chapter ahead can be useful to the reader.

2. Be Objective

Scientific communication should be based on logical and rational discourse. A common error researchers make is to try to 'sell' their findings or research. As a scientist, you are supposed to objectively evaluate, not advertise. Pointing out drawbacks or possible problems with your approach is good and, indeed, necessary; but raving about the wonderful work you have done is unscientific. You can *still* show how wonderful it is, but do this by using comparisons or rational arguments. Also, avoid emotive words such as 'wonderful', 'ghastly' and 'horrid'.

3. Support your Facts

Your writing can, and should, make statements of fact. Only a handful of statements can be made without support on the basis of universal acceptance (e.g. 'most people have two legs' or 'day alternates with night'). All other statements should be supported by either a line of reasoning (based on your results and logical conclusions), or by a reference to the work of a previous researcher (e.g. 'As Naicker (1988) has shown, gweedledidgets are orthogonally centroid.'). In the next chapter we will discuss how to handle such references.

4. Be Concise

Avoid woolly phrases and unnecessary words. Omit qualifiers such as 'quite', 'really' or 'in fact'. 'The reason that he went home was that it was raining' could, for example, be revised to 'He went home because it was raining'.

5. Be Definite

Avoid imprecise, unqualified terms such as 'nice', 'good', 'big' and 'fast'. Rather use exact measures or comparisons (e.g. 'it takes 7 milliseconds' or 'it is the same size as a gweedledidget').

6. One Paragraph, One Idea

A single paragraph should contain a single idea. Avoid overly long paragraphs (more than 500 words) if possible; your writing will be clearer and easier to read if the paragraphs are crisp and concise.

7. KISS

KISS (Keep It Simple, Stupid) is a good approach to any communication. Do not overelaborate.

8. Be Active and Use Short Verbs

Where possible, prefer the active to the passive. 'The workers consulted management' rather than 'Management was consulted by the workers'. Also, try to use short verbs rather than long phrases. Avoid 'The workers actioned a consultation with management'.

9. Eschew Obfuscatory Nomenclature

Don't use big words for their own sake! Some people believe that the most accurate word should always be used; some people just like fancy sounding words such as 'nascent', 'vitiate', 'opine' or 'symposiastic'. Extreme accuracy or fancy words might sound reasonable, but if most of your readers don't understand such words, then you are hardly communicating effectively. Also confusing are TLAs that your reader is unfamiliar with (three-letter acronyms, what else?).

10. Use Appropriate Terms

Use the technical terms appropriate to the field of research. This may seem to contradict the caution against using 'big words', but again it's a question of the audience – you have a right to expect readers of a paper on advanced calculus, for example, to be familiar with the terms and symbols of calculus. Having to define all basic terms at the beginning of reports would make the reports impractically long. At the same time, any terms that are *not* basic and could be misinterpreted by a fellow researcher in the field, *should* be defined.

11. I am not Worthy

The words 'I' and 'my' should be used very sparingly (some people would say not at all) in theses. If you present a valid argument, then you can make conclusions without using statements like 'I think that ...' or 'it is my opinion that ...'. If you *have* to give a personal opinion that is not fully supported, then use 'the author', e.g. 'the author concluded that ...'.

12. Use only Appropriate Authorities

When you use the work of someone else to support a statement, ensure that the person is an authority on the subject. For example, a politician's comment on a practical aspect of engineering is probably not of much academic worth; neither is a prince's comment on architecture. Your references and support should come from those who are authorities in the particular field rather than just respected individuals.

13. Be Careful with the 'Truth'

Never state a particular religious, political or humanistic world view as a truth (i.e. a fact). The fact that you believe or even *know* something to be so, still does not allow you to state it as a fact without reference or proof.

14. Avoid Anecdotes

An anecdotal style is a sure way to get your writing ignored. 'Little stories' from personal experience to illustrate points do not belong in a scientific document.

12.2 TURNING WORDS INTO PRINT: TYPOGRAPHICAL CONSIDERATIONS

At some stage, you will have to take your research and produce a document for the whole world to see. There is no such thing as the 'right' style for such a document. We list here some of the issues that you need to be concerned with. If you are uncertain whether a particular style is appropriate for your writing, consult your supervisor or promoter. What is extremely important, however, is that, once you have chosen a particular style, you use this style *consistently*.

Technology

You should use a **word processor** to type a manuscript, thesis or dissertation. Apart from the extra features a word processor provides (e.g. spelling checks), you can revise your work easily and quickly, and distribute the document electronically. Use a letter-quality printer (laser, ink-jet or similar) for final copies. (Although some dot-matrix printers are advertised as being 'near letter-quality' and produce fairly acceptable originals, photostatted copies do not look very good.)

Fonts

The **font** determines the shape of the letters you read. This font is Swiss. This font is Times Roman. The font for the body text (as opposed to that for various headings, footnotes and so on) is normally a standard font such as Courier New or New Century Schoolbook. Avoid the use of ornate fonts such as Gothic, Old English and *script fonts*. While they may look impressive, they are hard on the eye.

Most people use a font size of 12 points ('normal' typewriter size) for body text. Spacing between lines should be between one and one and a half, since both too little and too much white space between lines makes the text hard to read.

Headings

There are many options for headings and subheadings. Different fonts, font sizes, bold-face, text justification (left, right or centre) and (occasionally) underlining can all be effective. One possible system is to have chapter headings centred in large bold capitals, section headings left-justified in bold lower case, and subheadings left-justified in lower-case italics. Pick a system *you* feel comfortable with, and use it consistently.

Emphasis

If you want to stress a particular word or phrase, use *italics* or **bold**. Underlining is also an option, but it tends to cramp the surrounding text and distract the eye. Using exclamation marks to emphasise points can look!!! silly!!! and should be done very sparingly, and not at all in a truly scientific document.

Quotes

Direct quotes should be placed in quotation marks. The use of either single or double quote pairs is acceptable, e.g. Le Roux stated "Nihilism is nothing to be worried about", or Zuma remarks 'Mind over matter is a matter of the mind', although a common rule is 'single quotes first; doubles inside singles'. Obviously, you must give a reference for direct quotes. Note that you must copy a quote exactly, even if it contains an error. You can indicate that the source was in error, rather than it being your mistake, by inserting '[*sic*]' where the error occurs.

Widows and Orphans

A **widow** is the last line of a paragraph that sits by itself at the top of a page, while an **orphan** is the first line of a paragraph that sits by itself at the bottom of a page. You should avoid both of these. In particular, a heading or subheading must be followed on the same page by at least two lines of the section it heads.

Orphans are easily removed by inserting a page break before the paragraph; widows can take considerably more manipulation. Worry about this *only* when you are *absolutely* sure everything else is done – spending hours perfecting a document and then remembering you have to insert one more paragraph, which of course plays havoc with all your repairs, is not a pleasant experience (sigh).

If you are interested in more detailed discussions of and information about the subject of scientific writing, look at Arn84, Bor78, Ber71, Cam90, Chi82, Day89, Jut94 and Por94.

Discussion Questions and Exercises

1. Study the first two paragraphs of this chapter. Do you think they follow the guidelines for scientific writing given in the rest of the chapter? Rewrite them so that an audience of ten-year-olds could understand them.

2. Read a newspaper editorial. What features of the writing would you consider to be unscientific?

3. Write a half-page report on the Apollo 11 mission, using at least three sources of information. (You may need to visit your library to do this.) Your intended audience should be your fellow students. Is your finished report an example of scientific writing?

Chapter 13

Referencing

A requirement of scientific writing is that whenever you use results reported by other people or directly quote their work, you inform your reader as to exactly where you obtained the material. This is known as **referencing**. Such information includes the name of the author(s) of the work, the title of the work, where it was published and the date of publication. In this chapter, we discuss why referencing is important, as well as different methods of referencing.

13.1 WHY REFERENCE?

There are a number of reasons why correct referencing is vital. The most important are as follows:

- *To create credibility.* Saying 'I read somewhere that someone said that . . .' is not as likely to be believed as saying 'J. A. Tipworth stated in his book, *South African Fungi* (1990), that . . .'. More importantly, readers who want to *check* whether something was in fact said, or if a result was in fact reported, can do so only if they have access to the details of the publication.
- *To acknowledge credit.* If someone else's work was useful for your own work, that input obviously deserves to be acknowledged. By referencing, you not only give credit where it is due, but you also avoid the risk of someone thinking that you are falsely representing somebody else's work as your own. (This form of scientific cheating is called 'plagiarism', and gets severely punished.)
- *To direct readers to related research.* If particular sources were useful to you, then they are likely to be of interest to your readers. References provide valuable pointers to further information. This is why researchers give extensive details of the sources of the information they refer to.

13.2 REFERENCES AND REFERENCE LISTS

Giving full information on every occasion an author makes a reference would lead to clumsy and awkward writing. This is a hypothetical example:

> A number of reports – *Diverse Ditches* by A. J. Fruit, M. E. Vegetable and I. C. Mineral, published in Cape Town in 1991 by Juta; *Deeper Digging* by M. V. Harley, J. P. Yamaha, C. S. Vespa and Z. X. Suzuki published in *The International Journal of*

Building Science, volume 4, number 42, 1990; and *Delving Down* by I. B. Dammed, published in New York in 1993 by McGraw-Hill – all claim that ....'

If you consider that scientific writing can contain as many as 20 or more references on a page, it is clear that the above style is not practical. Instead, authors use a form of 'shorthand'. They insert a short code in the text where the reference occurs (**the point of reference**), and give a list of codes and their explanations (**the reference list**) at the end of the report. In the reference list, the full publishing information of the document appears next to each code. Some common systems for these codes are discussed later in this chapter.

Source Lists, Bibliographies and Reference Lists

A **source** is anything you used in compiling your writing – books, journal papers, conference proceedings, personal communications, talks you've heard, newspaper articles and so forth. A **source list** gives all the sources used. The term **bibliography** is often used as a synonym for source list; strictly speaking, though, a bibliography contains only books. A **reference list** give only those sources that have been referenced (cited) in the text – if you've read something but haven't referred to it in your own writing, it does *not* appear in a reference list.

Books can contain source lists, bibliographies, reference lists or combinations of the three; theses, dissertations and papers normally contain only reference lists.

13.3 SYSTEMS FOR MAKING REFERENCES

A reference system specifies the format of the code used for the reference in the text, and how the reference list is constructed.

Several reference systems are available, none of which is more 'right' than another. Many disciplines favour a particular system, although two journals in the same discipline can still have totally different referencing systems as their standard formats. However, the point to remember is that if you are sending something you have written to a particular journal that insists that all authors use a particular reference system, then you must fulfil that requirement. We discuss three common systems here.

The Harvard System

This system, also known as the 'Oxford system', is the most widely used, and is the norm for the human sciences. Here the reference is in parentheses, and includes the author's name, date of publication and page number(s). For example, '(Foster, 1989:120)' or '(Maharaj, 1992:15–19)'. Omit page numbers if your reference is to the work as a whole.

When the work referred to is by two authors, give both names in the reference, e.g. '(Masondo and Mills, 1993:21–2)'. When there are more than two authors, the first author's name is given followed by the abbreviation '*et al.*', which literally means 'and others', e.g. '(Einstein *et al.*, 1955:42)'. Often, the code itself is sufficient for the reader to identify the source.

In the case where an author produced two or more works in a year, letters of the alphabet are added to distinguish between the works. For example, suppose you refer to two of Redfield's works, both written in 1988, then there would be two distinct references ' (Redfield, 1988a)' and '(Redfield, 1988b)' to avoid confusion. These works would obviously be listed in the reference list using the same letters of the alphabet.

The FTL (first three letters) System

This system tries to reduce the 'clumsiness' of references in the Harvard system, while retaining the useful information in the reference. References consist of the first three letters of the (first) author's name, followed by the last two digits of the year of publication. For example, a reference that in the Harvard system is written as '(Manning and Munsamy, 1952)' is written in the FTL system as '(Man52)'.

In the case of a clash (authors of two or more different works in the same year with the same first three letters of names), letters of the alphabet are added to distinguish between the works. For example, suppose Redfield and Reddy had both written works in 1988, then there would be two distinct references '(Red88a)' and '(Red88b)' to avoid confusion. The same applies to referencing two works by the same author in the same year.

The Numerical System

Much beloved by engineering journals, this system ensures the 'smoothest' referencing, but at the cost of providing little information at the point of reference. References are given as numbers inside square brackets, e.g. '[12]'. In one version of this system, items are numbered in the order in which they are first referenced in the text; in another, the items are numbered alphabetically. Whichever version is used, a source only appears once in the reference list (just as with the other systems described above), while all references in the text of the work use the same number as code.

13.4 THE REFERENCE LIST

The system you use does not affect the reference list, apart from determining whether it is ordered alphabetically or numerically, and what the first item in a list entry is – this is identical to the reference itself, but often without brackets or page numbers. There are different approaches to the reference list. Suggested reference-list entries for some common sources of information are given below.

Books

For a book, after the names and initials of all author(s) and the date of publication come the title, the city of publication and the publisher, e.g. a FTL-referenced list could include the entry:

Bun91 Bunter, B. B. and Badger, E. B., 1991. *Modern Movements*. London: Wiley.

You can (usually) find the information you need to produce the reference on the first few pages of a book, before the text begins. If you want to reference an article within a book written by someone other than the author, just use the word 'in' before the book details. For example, using the numeric system and wanting to reference an article by Zappa that appears in a book edited by Kruger, you would have:

[17] Zappa, F. A., 1978. Why censorship is good. In Kruger, J. (ed.), *The Joy of Mindless Moralising*. Durban: Butterworths.

Note that the abbreviation (ed.) indicates the editor of a book, and (eds) indicates editors. The abbreviation 'edn' indicates the edition of a book.

Journals

A journal or magazine article is referenced as follows: Name of author(s), date, title of article, name of journal, volume number, issue number (if the volume is divided up into issues), pages where the article appears. The journal name is normally italicised. Three possible ways of making a reference list entry for an article appearing on pages 108 to 112 of the journal *Diseases of the Nervous System* are as follows:

Mahole, S. A., 1994. Drug abuse and memory. *Diseases of the Nervous System*, vol. 29, no. 10, pp. 108–112.

Mahole, S. A., 1994. Drug abuse and memory. *Diseases of the Nervous System*, **29**(10), 108–112.

Mahole, S. A. Drug abuse and memory. *Dis. Nerv. Sys.* **29**:**10** (1994), 108–112.

The third example above makes use of an approved standard abbreviation for the journal name – you should never make up your own abbreviations. Some fields commonly use standard abbreviations; others avoid these sometimes cryptic abbreviations. Whatever method you choose to employ, be *consistent*. (Remember, however, that some journals insist on a particular system, and if they do, you must use that system.)

Conference Proceedings

If the paper has been published in the conference proceedings, make the reference in the following form:

Nep92 Nepal, T., 1992. Big bytes for the apple. In T. Zondo (ed.), *Proceedings of the 4th International Symposium on Information Technology*, pp. 89–95. London: Oxford University Press.

If the paper has not been published as part of the conference proceedings, then the following form is common:

Lin, W., 1990. TLAs: Are three-letter acronyms a help or a hindrance? Paper presented at Linguistics 90, 4th Annual Conference of Linguistics and Meaning, Monterey, California, October.

Theses and Dissertations

You will also have to reference other theses or dissertations (T/Ds). It does not matter what level the T/D is. A typical entry is as follows:

[32] Paarman, J. T., 1983. An Investigation of Gastric Compensation. Unpublished doctoral dissertation, University of Durban-Westville.

People

When referring to a communication or correspondence with someone (normally only referenced if the individual is an authority in the field), the individual's name, the date of the communication, the individual's affiliation and the expression 'personal communication' abbreviated to 'pers. comm.' are often given as the reference entry. For example, such a reference would look like this in the FTL system:

Kha01 Khan, M. I., 2001, University of Nairobi, pers. comm.

An alternative style is not to include personal communications in the reference list, but to give all the information at the point of reference instead.

The Internet

The rules for referencing a website are still being formulated. One reasonable approach is to provide the most natural but general URL, e.g. www.tug.org. Being very specific can be a problem, as people tend to restructure and revise their website on a regular basis.

There are many types of sources; those mentioned above are just the more commonly used ones. If you are unsure of how to reference a particular item, check with your advisor. Examples of the reference systems described in this chapter can be found in Appendix A.

Discussion Questions and Exercises

1. Which of the three systems above do you prefer? Why?

2. Journal papers typically have more references per page than books do. Why should this be so?

3. One of the problems in the previous chapter was to write a half-page report using at least three sources. Reference this report using any of the three systems described above.

4. Say you read an article by Mey in which she quotes (and references) Edwards as saying 'The real answer is 42'. You want to use this quotation yourself. How would you reference it? How would someone obtaining the quote from your report reference it?

Chapter 14

Standard Report Formats

This chapter describes common formats for theses and dissertations, proposals to conduct research and company reports. Formats are used as a standard style of presenting information, but by themselves do not guarantee effective communication – this is still *your* job.

14.1 THE THESIS OR DISSERTATION

Layout

A typical thesis or dissertation (T/D) is presented on A4-size paper and has the following elements, in the order given:

1. *The title page.* This normally contains the title of the T/D, the full name of the author, and a statement along the lines of 'Submitted in partial fulfilment of the requirements for the (degree name) in the Department of (department name), (institution).' At the bottom of the title page might appear the city in which the institution is found and the date of the T/D's acceptance, together with copyright.
2. *The preface.* This details where the work was carried out (e.g. Department of Computer Studies, ML Sultan Technikon), under whose supervision it was done, and over what period the research was conducted. A statement of originality should also appear, along the lines of 'These studies represent original work by the author and have not been submitted in any form to any other tertiary institution. Where use has been made of the work of others, it has been duly acknowledged in the text.'
3. *Acknowledgements.* This page allows the author to acknowledge contributions made to the T/D by others. It is normal to acknowledge the work of one's mentors, any institutions or organisations that have provided funding or assistance, and the active help of anyone directly involved with the T/D (research colleagues and assistants, typists, proofreaders). Acknowledgements of a personal nature (e.g. to parents, spouses) are common, but should be brief.
4. *The abstract.* The abstract should give, in as concise a way as possible, an outline or summary of the T/D. It should be short and exact – an abstract of longer than 25 lines is unusual. The abstract should be the last piece of the thesis that is finalised.
5. *A table of contents.* See pages iii–vi of this book for an example of a table of contents. There is also sometimes a list of figures or tables.

6. *The body of the T/D.* The chapters in the T/D now follow. The first chapter is generally an **introduction.** This highlights what the subsequent chapters contain, includes a brief overview of previous work in the field and gives definitions of important terms. The last chapter is normally a **conclusion**, which summarises the previous chapters in a far more detailed manner than the abstract, and includes indications of what future research is necessary in the field, and why. The chapters in between contain the report on the actual research conducted.
7. *The reference list.* See the previous chapter for details.
8. *Appendices.* These are often numbered A, B, C, etc., and contain anything that the T/D uses that is not in its chapters. Computer listings, derivations of formulas, the raw data from which information used in the T/D was derived, etc., are often contained in appendices rather than in the body of the T/D.

Page Numbering, Headers and Footers

Page numbers must be included. These normally appear at either the bottom centre or the top right of the page. Headers (at the top of the page) or footers (at the bottom) giving the T/D or chapter title are sometimes included.

Note that the pages comprising items 1 to 5 above are normally numbered using roman numerals (i, ii, iii, etc.). At the start of the body of the T/D, the page number is reset to 1, and numbering from this point on uses Arabic numerals (1, 2, 3, etc.).

Length

There is no correct length for a T/D. It is possible for a 20-page T/D to be too long and for a 500-page T/D to be too short. The length of the T/D is determined by the problem, the discipline, and the ease or difficulty of reporting on the research. Whether you have 'done enough' is a question you should address together with your supervisor, but remember that 'enough' here refers to enough research and an effective write-up of this research, not to any set number of pages.

Figures, Tables and Equations

Figures should be clear, and preferably printed. If not printed, they should be drawn using Indian ink. If you need a figure that cannot be easily produced on an A4 page, then it should be folded to A4 size and pasted onto a blank A4 page so that the reader can unfold it.

All figures and tables should be numbered (e.g. Figure 1, Table 2) so that they can be referred to in the text. (If they *are not* referred to in the text, then they shouldn't be in the T/D in the first place!) Figure/table numbers normally appear centred or left-aligned below the figure/table, followed by a brief but useful description of the figure/table (i.e. the title of the figure/table). For example, 'Table 1: Cumulative carbon readings (1960–1980)' or 'Figure 3: Internal structure of a glockenspiel'.

Equations can be numbered. If so, equation numbers often appear next to the equation in parentheses without any description, such as:

'$e = mc^2$ (5)'.

Footnotes

Use footnotes sparingly, as they tend to break the reader's concentration. Many writers maintain that if something is worth mentioning at all, then it is worth mentioning in the text itself (i.e. there should be no footnotes). Some disciplines, however, are wedded to footnotes (and use them for references).

Margins

A typical margin size on A4 paper is 25 mm for all four margins (top, bottom, right and left). Avoid margins a lot narrower than this (as it causes text to seem very cramped) or a lot wider than this (as it causes text to look 'lost in space'). Check with printers/binders whether you need to leave extra space on the left margin for binding.

Binding

Final copies of a T/D should be professionally bound. In some institutions, it is usual to submit the T/D to the examiners unbound, so that any revisions the examiners suggest can be incorporated into final copies. Check your own institution's policy.

Concluding Remarks

In this section we discussed style points you must consider when writing a thesis or dissertation, and gave examples of various acceptable styles, formats and techniques. Remember that these serve only as guidelines; if the particular circumstances of your T/D call for a different format, then use that format. Always check with your supervisor to ensure that the style you use will be acceptable. Above all, after you have made a particular choice, stick with it throughout the T/D. Consistency is essential in scientific writing, and will be appreciated by all your readers – some of whom will be your examiners.

14.2 PROPOSALS TO CONDUCT RESEARCH

There are two areas in which **research proposals** are necessary. One is when you draw up a research proposal for a masters or doctoral thesis/dissertation, and the other is when you draw up a proposal as part of an application for funding. The former document will be studied by the faculty research committee and (possibly) the institutional research committee; the latter document will be studied by potential funders such as funding bodies (e.g. the NRF or MRC) or industry. Although both types of proposal cover much the same ground, they will be addressed to different *audiences*, and therefore should be compiled with this in mind.

Many research proposals are drawn up according to a set format devised by the institution or the funding body. *Use that format*. It might be awkward, clumsy and unfriendly, but those who judge the proposal are certain to react unfavourably if you ignore a format that they have specified.

Funding bodies often provide their own proposal forms that you have to complete. A common error in filling out such forms is to write something like 'see attached document' in response to a specific question. Rather summarise your attached document in answer to the question, and then put 'see attached document for greater detail'. Review committees often have many applications before them, and forcing the members to scratch around to find material can have a negative effect (and there is also no guarantee that your attached documents have all been copied and distributed).

Proposals for research funding must include a **budget**. Budgets should be inclusive and realistic. Include all items that will cost money, down to stationery and computer disks. Sometimes you will be unsure of the cost of a particular item, e.g. the cost of a hotel room in New York for the conference you plan to attend. In these cases, justify your budget cost on some generally accepted basis. For the example above, you might use the daily subsistence allowance recommended by your institution. It is a mistake to artificially inflate a budget. Some people do this on the grounds that 'all budgets get cut, so if I ask for double what I need I'll wind up getting the right amount'. Not only is this dishonest, but there is also a good chance you will be refused any grant.

A check-list of items you should include in a research proposal appears below – remember, though, that if a specific format is provided, you should stick to it:

- the proposed title of the research;
- the researcher's name;
- the researcher's co-worker(s)/supervisor(s);
- a statement of the research problem;
- a brief background to the problem;

- a brief description of the research methods to be employed;
- possible outcomes of the research (i.e. why it is worth doing); and
- a description of the proposed reporting of the research, e.g. papers, company reports and/or a dissertation/thesis. (Some institutions require a rough chapter outline for dissertation/thesis proposals.)

14.3 COMPANY REPORTS

Commissioned research, where a company pays you to do research in order to solve a particular problem, has some distinct reporting features. These include the following:

- *Be considerate to top management.* Executives are busy people, and while the R & D (research and development) workers in an organisation may welcome the opportunity to read through every line of your 300-page report, most executives will not have the time or the inclination to do so. Company reports should therefore begin with an **executive summary**, i.e. a page or at most two that summarises the most important aspects of the problem involved and the solution you found.
- *Agree to agree.* In any commissioned research, you should agree to (and sign) exact specifications of what is to be researched and how this is to be done, before commencing the work. This prevents disagreements as to whether you have done what you undertook to do, and precludes people from 'moving the goalposts' as your work progresses. These exact specifications should appear as the first section of your report, immediately after the executive summary and the table of contents.
- *They name the child.* Don't create your own title for the research report. Companies have their own systems for classifying and filing their reports, and so you must obtain the title of your report (which could be something on the lines of CA712-14-X) from the company.

Discussion Questions and Exercises

1. Get a copy of a thesis or dissertation (any one will do) from your library. Does the format conform to the specifications given above?

2. Find out what format is used for research proposals at your institution.

3. Consider what the different audiences would be for research proposals, theses/dissertations and company reports. Would this affect the type of language you could use in the reports? How?

4. Get a paper from a journal, cover up the abstract and read the paper. Then write an appropriate abstract. Compare your effort with the actual abstract.

Part 5

BROADER ISSUES IN RESEARCH

Research affects the world, and researchers should be aware of the possible effects of their research on the world. In this part, we discuss some of the social and ethical considerations relevant to research, as well as describing the development of scientific thought in human civilisation.

In Chapter 15 we focus on the issues of ethics and intellectual honesty; in Chapter 16 we describe the evolution of scientific thought; and in Chapter 17 we discuss the role of research in South Africa's reconstruction and development.

Chapter 15

Research Issues

Research carries with it responsibilities. A researcher has responsibilities to fellow researchers, to any participants in the research, to society as a whole and, most importantly, to her/himself. In this chapter we consider some of the issues and ethical questions that may arise in research. In many cases, there are conflicting views on a particular issue, and all we can do is to explain some of the arguments on each side. As a researcher, you will have to think about these issues yourself, and come to your own conclusions about them.

15.1 ETHICAL QUESTIONS

There are two fundamental ethical questions in research: what are morally acceptable research topics, and what are morally acceptable methods to research a particular topic? Both questions, as with most moral issues, have been and continue to be the subjects of considerable debate, and therefore cannot be finally answered in this book.

As a researcher, you should be aware of these issues, and *always* consider the effects of your research before you start it. If in doubt, you can consult your promoter/supervisor, or refer the problem to the ethics committee at your institution (often a substructure of the research committee) for expert guidance.

Dubious Subjects for Research

> *'Beauty is truth, truth beauty,' – that is all*
> *Ye know on earth, and all ye need to know.*
> (John Keats, 'Ode on a Grecian Urn')

One school of thought holds that all knowledge is good, and therefore there should be no 'taboo' subjects. At first glance this may seem attractive to the scientifically inclined. Some might not see why there is an argument at all. If you fall into this group, consider how you would feel about people conducting research into the following questions:

- Are black people more or less intelligent than white people?
- How regularly do children masturbate?
- What relationships are there between physical characteristics ('looks') and career success?
- How does one clone a human being?
- How does one make an atomic bomb?

All five questions have resulted in published research, and the first three are discussed in Jor89, Lou91 and Bar94. But for many people, one or more of these questions should not have been the subject of research in the first place. Decide for yourself whether all knowledge is good, or whether there are topics that are inherently wrong to research.

Dubious Ways of Researching

Research may be well designed and procedurally correct, and yet can be ethically flawed. Perhaps examples are the best way to show this.

> *J. B. Watson, the 'father' of behaviourism, conducted a series of tests in which a baby was subjected to a loud noise (to scare it) every time it saw a particular toy animal (Wel38). Not surprisingly, the baby eventually became afraid of the toy even in the absence of the noise, and in fact became conditioned to fear a range of other toy animals. Something was proved about conditioning responses – but was it ethically acceptable to do this to a baby?*

> *Carson and Butcher (Car92) report a 1950 study by Keys where conscientious objectors were used to study the effect of food deprivation on humans. After being placed on famine rations for six months, the subjects had an average weight loss of 24%, and various mood and temperamental effects were recorded. In other words, the research caused human beings to suffer.*

The above two cases of research involving human beings would not be approved by ethics committees today. One criterion used to measure whether a research project is ethically acceptable is that of 'informed consent': only volunteers, in full possession of the facts about the research project, can be used as subjects of the research. This is expected to apply even if there is no chance of the subjects being harmed.

Of course, while humans are in a position to give informed consent, animals are not. It is accepted practice to use animals for a wide variety of clinical tests, examples of which include:

- the exposure of animals to extreme amounts of cigarette smoke to see if cancers result;
- the exposure of animals to a wide range of products intended for use on humans, from drugs to shampoos, to check for adverse reactions; and
- the use of healthy animals to test new surgical procedures (e.g. heart transplants).

Those people who are against harming animals during research (called 'anti-vivisectionists') maintain that animals have rights too, and that such experimentation constitutes unacceptable cruelty to animals. They maintain that the world has enough shampoos, cosmetics and the like already, and so there is no need to continually rub new products into animals' eyes to see the effect. Furthermore, even when such experimentation may be thought necessary, they believe that the living conditions of the animals and the experimentation methods used are often unnecessarily cruel.

All this might be appealing reasoning, but people who support such research ask: 'Would you like things to be tested on humans first rather than animals?'. If you answer 'yes' to this question, then would you be happy for your mother to be the 'guinea-pig' when a new drug is first tested?

For an in-depth discussion of this controversy, you might contrast the views of Fox86 with those of Lan89.

Dubious Results

A particularly vexing question is what to do with the results of morally unacceptable research. In the early 1940s, Nazi 'scientists' performed ghastly human experimentation on prisoners that produced data about such things as castration, sterilisation, pain thresholds and operations without anaesthetic (Ast85). Clearly, the research was ethically unacceptable, but given that it has been done, and that the methods used were otherwise scientifically correct, should not the resulting data be used? You decide!

15.2 INTELLECTUAL HONESTY

Apart from considering the ethics of the research topics and of the research methods used, a researcher is expected to be ethically correct in a number of other ways. Foremost on this list is that the researcher is honest: honest about the methods, honest about the results and honest about who did the work.

Plagiarism is the unacknowledged use of the work of someone else, where the researcher claims credit for work that he/she has not done. Careful referencing (see Chapter 13) should ensure that you do not plagiarise by accident – remember, it cannot be plagiarism if you *acknowledge* where you got the information. Plagiarism might be a tempting way to avoid hard work – but, if it is discovered and proven, it will mean the end of your scientific career and, in cases of masters and doctoral students, will lead not only to the retraction of the degree, but also to expulsion from the institution concerned.

Good scientists accept the results they get, for they are interested in knowledge. Occasionally, bad scientists falsify results, for they are interested in fame or in 'proving' a particular point of view. Many of these frauds are irritating, but do not affect the world at large; however, some of these frauds have set scientific advancement back many years. One famous fraud was the Piltdown Man (Wei80). In 1912, Charles Dawson announced the discovery of a skull with a mixture of human and apelike features. This provided scholars with the much-sought-after 'missing link' in human evolution. It was only in 1953 that tests proved that the parts of the skull were only a few hundred years old and that the skull was an elaborate forgery. The missing link was again missing, and scientists had to rethink their results.

One reassuring aspect of this issue is that the nature of scientific enquiry ensures that fraud will always be found out when later results reveal inconsistencies. A researcher has the obligation to expose scientific fraud wherever it is found.

Closely aligned with falsifying results is the selective choice of data. This happens when researchers do not present all the data they captured, but only that which supports their preferred hypothesis. Often this is not done as a deliberate fraud; rather, the researcher, on seeing unexpected data, reasons on the lines of: 'Oh, that can't be. There must have been something wrong with my equipment/experiment/subject. Better omit that data from my report.' This is unacceptable, and could, in fact, lead to very important data being ignored. If there is a genuine concern about the validity of data, it is acceptable to omit it from consideration if – and only if – you state in your report that you have done so, and give the reasons for doing so. If space constraints allow, such data could also be presented in raw form (i.e. as actual results rather than summaries) in an appendix to your report.

15.3 INTELLECTUAL PROPERTY RIGHTS

We have already observed that copying other people's writing without acknowledgement is plagiarism, and cannot be defended. The same issues are involved in using pirated software and copying pictures and sound clips without permission, but there are many who argue that piracy is acceptable. What we would like to consider here is *your* **intellectual property rights**: i.e. who owns the results of your work?

Our experiences suggest that South African tertiary institutions have a poorly defined policy on intellectual property rights. In particular, they do not confront the issue of who owns work done by students. We would like to suggest the following policy. Copyright of theses, research, etc., performed by a student should remain with the author, but the institution should be given a royalty-free license for internal educational purposes. You may wish to check with the research office at your institution about its policy towards work you have done. If you do research explicitly for a company, and are paid for it, then it is reasonable that the company owns your research.

Discussion Questions and Exercises

1. Given that a particular society has moral qualms about abortion, should tissue from aborted foetuses be used in medical research in that society?

2. Genetic engineering has now reached a stage where it is possible to 'design' features into plants and animals. There is a proposal to develop a new type of cow that has no legs but produces vast quantities of milk. Is there an ethical question involved in such a situation? What do you think?

3. While most people agree that Watson's experiments on conditioning in children would not be accepted by a research ethics committee today, there are no qualms about using his results. Is this reasonable?

Chapter 16

The History and Philosophy of Research

People have searched for answers to questions about the nature, meaning and purpose of life since the beginning of known civilisation. Why this continual search? The reasons are hotly debated by philosophers (see Kea86 for more details), but many attribute this search for knowledge to the notion that knowledge empowers. Sir Francis Bacon wrote that 'There is a most intimate connection and almost an identity between the ways of human power and human knowledge' (Far53). Such empowerment is present in all aspects of our existence – the skilled technician, the graduate, the company that knows how to produce a superior product, the country that knows how to create wealth, and so on.

In this chapter, we look at how the search for knowledge has developed through history, paying particular attention to the ongoing debate about what knowledge is and how it may be reliably obtained. As current scientific research across the world is rooted in a line of development traceable back to the ancient Greeks, we begin with them.

16.1 GREEK THOUGHT AND THE ORIGINS OF RESEARCH

From about 600 B.C., the ancient Greeks contributed significantly to the process of how humankind searches for knowledge. This contribution provided the roots of current-day science and research.

Greek civilisation at the time was itself the product of earlier thought. Written language in particular had been developed earlier by the ancient Egyptians and Babylonians. It is known that by 3000 B.C., both cultures possessed written logographic languages (Gro95). The possession of a language consisting of symbols rather than mere pictures meant that any knowledge acquired could be passed down from generation to generation, rather than having to be 'relearnt' by each succeeding generation. There is dispute as to the nature of further contributions by the Egyptians and Babylonians. Some maintain that their contribution to human knowledge was in the form of 'rules of thumb' regarding agriculture, mathematics, astronomy and medicine, motivated purely by practical necessity (see Rus91 and Far53). Others suggest that they also showed original and abstract thought (Far53).

While other early civilisations made similar advances, it is unclear to what extent these influenced ancient Greek thought and therefore modern views on research.

Pre-Socratic Thought

Western philosophy began with Thales (c. 585 B.C.) (Rus91). From the point of view of the history of research, his importance is that he asked a **question** (All66). The question itself, which was along the lines of 'What is the source of all things?' and his answer, 'The source of all things is water', are not important. However, his question sparked a debate amongst his contemporaries that initiated the ancient Greek quest for knowledge. Some of the attempts to answer Thales' question relied on mysticism and religion. However, as early as Heraclitus (c. 480 B.C.), there was an attempt to **observe** nature in order to come up with a **common-sense** approach to answering the question, rather than rely on the deities to provide the answer (Far53). With Pythagoras (c. 550 B.C.), hailed as the founder of modern science (Fle84), we see the beginnings of **speculative hypotheses** and **deduction**. Atomists such as Democritus (5th century B.C.) also attempted a more **scientific** and **rational** approach to the question of the nature of things.

Socrates, Plato and Aristotle

Socrates (c. 470–399 B.C.), who is known primarily through the writings of his pupil, Plato (c. 428–348 B.C.) (Rus91), developed what became known as the **Socratic method**. This method is basically a **dialectical** process, whereby a thesis or argument is presented, an antithesis or counter argument is then presented, and from this comes a synthesis of this opposition of ideas comprising new knowledge. This in turn becomes the thesis for a new dialectical process, and so on. Plato was **idealistic** in his approach to the question of reality. He saw reality as existing not in the material world, but in ideas (i.e. in the perfect forms of things conceived of by the mind). Plato's pupil, Aristotle (384–322 B.C.), on the other hand, was **realistic** in his approach. For Aristotle, reality consisted of material, individual things and he placed great emphasis on the role of observation in acquiring knowledge. The first attempts at **categorisation** can also be seen in Aristotle's work (Rus91). Aristotle's categories were classes that described different 'modes of being', e.g. substance, relation, quantity and quality. Aristotle's most significant contribution to knowledge is his formulation of the **syllogism**, a form of argument in which, if something is stated, something else is logically true (Fle84). The creation of the syllogism led to **deductive logic**.

Post-Socratic Thought

Other schools of thought followed on from Plato and Aristotle. **Hedonism**, which is the idea that happiness is the proper goal of human actions, led to the belief that the pursuit of knowledge should concern itself only with what was practically useful. These views were clearly expressed in the ideas of the Cyrenaics and the Epicureans (4th century B.C.) (Fle84). The idea that **no sure knowledge** can be found makes an early appearance in the theories of the Sceptics (c. 280–80 B.C.) (Rus91). The contentious issue of a **moral basis** for the enquiry after knowledge appears strongly in the thought of the Sceptics (although it can be seen to varying degrees in the thought of Socrates, Plato and Aristotle).

From 300 B.C. to 400 A.D., although there were developments along existing lines of thought, no new ways of thinking developed in Greek thought. However, the Greeks became increasingly exposed to Eastern thought (Zoroastrian dualism, Buddhism, etc.) as a result of Alexander the Great's conquests.

With the decline of the Graeco-Roman civilisation from approximately 400 A.D. onwards, the only significant advances in science and scientific thought for some 800 years were those made by the Arabs in fields such as astronomy and algebra.

16.2 THE DEVELOPMENT OF MODERN SCIENTIFIC THOUGHT

It is only around the 13th century that one sees a resurgence of *new* developments in thought. This was made possible by the combined contributions of the monastic orders of the Christian church, which provided the structures for a revival of learning (i.e. schools), and the Arabs, who had preserved ancient Greek knowledge in libraries and also maintained the idea of education (Rus91, Gro95).

It was then that Thomas Aquinas (c. 1225) made the works of Aristotle known to the West. William of Occam (c. 1290) contributed by insisting that the pursuit of knowledge could occur without metaphysics or theology playing a role. This break from the church contributed to an intellectual climate that made possible the significant advances in thought that followed. Occam was also responsible for the idea that, when given a number of possible explanations for a phenomenon, the simplest one should be chosen. This is known in modern science as **Occam's razor**.

The Renaissance of Science

The rise of modern science begins with Copernicus (1473–1543). By introducing mathematical reasoning into cosmology, he came up with the theory that the earth revolves around the sun, and that the earth was not, as had been previously thought, the centre of the universe. Kepler (1571–1630) refined Copernicus' thought, and devised the three planetary laws of motion.

Galileo (1564–1642), sometimes called the founder of modern mechanics, refined the techniques of **experimentation** and **observation**. Consequently, he discovered the law of falling bodies and the law of inertia, and also published many new discoveries resulting from his telescopic observations. Galileo also argued for the separation of theology and science. Newton (1642–1727), in addition to formalising the three laws of motion, discovered the law of universal gravitation and contributed to the theory of light.

The theories of these four men (Copernicus, Kepler, Galileo and Newton) form the foundation of our modern scientific theories. It was Sir Francis Bacon (1561–1626) who identified, formalised and developed the method of thought that these four men were using, namely **inductive logic**. Until the 15th century, intellectual thought had been largely bound to deductive logic.

Descartes, Locke and Kant

Descartes (1596–1650) is said to be the founder of modern philosophy. He was unhappy with the way philosophical thought was conducted, and wanted to achieve the same degree of certainty in philosophy as was being achieved in the natural sciences. To this end he created his **method of doubt**: everything that is not absolutely certain is rejected, and what remains is simply expressed in his famous dictum, 'I think, therefore I am' (*Cogito ergo sum*). From this our knowledge is then rebuilt according to logical principles. Descartes' philosophy was hence highly **rationalistic**.

Locke (1632–1704) was the founder of **empiricism**. He claimed that all knowledge, with the possible exception of mathematics and logic, is derived from experience. At best, our general truths concerning the world can only be highly *probable* and not certain (Fle84). Locke stressed the importance of the senses in obtaining knowledge, while Descartes stressed the importance of reason for the same purpose.

Kant (1724–1804) made a strenuous attempt to reconcile various aspects of Descartes' and Locke's thought. Kant was extremely impressed with the advances made in the natural sciences. However, such science was presenting a highly **mechanistic** and **deterministic** picture of the world. Kant was concerned that this, if accepted as the true picture of reality, would be a denial of the individual's autonomy and freedom of will. He thus attempted, through a study of pure reason, to find out how enquiry becomes scientific. His conclusion (very simplistically!) was that we make progress in the search for knowledge when our experiments and observations are guided by certain rational principles (Kan46).

Continental Philosophy

Continental philosophy follows on from Descartes. Hegel (1770–1831) developed the idea of the dialectic further. With the development of **phenomenology** by Husserl (1859–1938) and Heidegger (1889–1976), there is a shift away from the attempt to find **meaning** in a 'narrow scientific attitude' (Kea86). Heidegger claimed that meaning was to be found in the fact that as humans we 'exist' in the world. This places emphasis on the role of the observer. Around this time, Einstein (1879–1955) formulated his theories of relativity, which were not only of tremendous importance for physics, but were also interesting from a philosophical viewpoint. Relativity implies that the **observer** is vitally important to the results of a scientific experiment, and that there is no such thing as a completely objective observer.

Later continental philosophy (such as existentialism, critical theory and structuralism) led to a greater stress on the role of individual creativity in scientific thought. Generally, the rejection of a narrow scientific attitude has led to a broader, less prescriptive interpretation of the search for knowledge. A prime example of this is the multidisciplinary approach.

British Philosophy

British philosophy developed from the empiricist ideas of Locke, with thinkers such as Berkeley (1685–1753) and Hume (1711–76). J. S. Mill (1806–73) founded **utilitarianism**, which is based on the theory that actions are judged on their consequences, and an action that produces 'good' (happiness, usefulness, etc.) is to be desired. **Logical positivism** stressed the importance of empiricism as a method of enquiry. The logical positivists attempted to systematise the empirical method with the use of various logical procedures such as the **verifiability principle.** Popper (1902–?) stressed that a single false result (**falsifiability criterion**) could show a theory to be false, while no number of positive results could *prove* it to be true, but could only add to our confidence in the theory.

The Uncertainty of Science

All of 20th-century science has been influenced by the development of quantum mechanics. Heisenberg made a critical contribution to quantum theory by showing that the position and the momentum of sub-atomic particles cannot be simultaneously determined (Heisenberg's **uncertainty principle**). Therefore, at a very basic level, and hence at all higher levels, all phenomena must have a degree of uncertainty. This fundamental uncertainty has profound implications for all of science and research. (For an excellent detailed discussion of the role of certainty in science, see Cas93.)

16.3 SOCIAL RESEARCH METHODS

As the title of this chapter indicates, it is mainly concerned with the history and philosophy of scientific research, and as such is unashamedly Euro-centric, simply because it is an historical fact that the scientific method was developed primarily in a European setting, or in settings with basic methodologies and philosophies that sprang largely from European sources (e.g. America).

This is not to deny the contribution of other civilisations and other research methods. There are a number of local texts in particular that focus on research in the social sciences from an African perspective. For a brief introduction to the academic investigation of social issues in Africa, see Ble00. The most comprehensive and challenging resource on the subject is the textbook Ter99.

16.4 RESEARCH TODAY

Most of the different ways of thinking (speculation, observation, deduction, etc.) that people use to acquire knowledge today had made an appearance by the 4th century A.D. The contributions of ancient civilisations are therefore vital: it is usually far more difficult to 'invent' something than it is to refine and develop it. However, it was only from about the 14th century onwards that these approaches were developed to the extent that rapid progress could be made by using them.

The 20th-century approach to research consists of a curious combination of the various approaches outlined above. Research must be rigorously and thoroughly carried out, and there are definite rules that researchers must comply with in order to produce results that are valid (e.g. logical and statistical rules). While researchers are always attempting to establish some theory as a 'fact' about the universe, there is at the same time a reluctance to call such facts 'truths'. There is a tendency amongst researchers to disbelieve that anything can be known to 100% certainty. The nature of both statistical techniques and quantum theory lends support to this viewpoint.

Researchers need to be aware that they are *part* of the research process. While researchers are expected to be objective, they will nevertheless influence this process in many ways. The researcher is an observer, and hence views the experiment or research from a unique position. In addition, depending on what the researcher's interests and background are, she will decide to research certain topics and not others, and to use one methodology of approaching a research problem rather than another.

Indeed, there is a growing tendency in philosophy towards a more individualistic and less absolute approach. Rorty argues that we should not look for a 'permanent framework for enquiry' (Ror80). Rather we should 'see knowing not as having an essence, to be described by scientists or philosophers, but rather as a right, by current standards, to believe ...'.

Discussion Questions and Exercises

1. 'Most of the philosophy described above is the product of dead white men and is no longer relevant.' Discuss.

2. Does the fact that everything is uncertain mean that there is nothing we can know?

Chapter 17

Research and South Africa's Needs

17.1 COUNTRY-SPECIFIC RESEARCH

Some argue that all research is good, and that research should be pursued for its own sake, free of intervention from government. On the other hand, some argue that the impact of the research on society should be considered, especially if society is footing the bill. A great deal of research at academic institutions is funded by the taxpayer, be it directly through government subsidies to the institutions involved or indirectly through government funding bodies such as the NRF and MRC. Why should the taxpayer pay for some academic indulging himself in researching a pet theory that has no significance for the country?

Some have argued that any research not geared towards solving specific problems in the country should not be supported, and that pure research in particular should be left to first-world countries 'who can afford it'. But, as we have seen, the distinction between pure and applied research is a tenuous one, and today's pure research can be, and often is, the basis of tomorrow's vital applied research. In addition, if all nations took the position that 'We'll just research our own problems, and let other research be somebody else's problem', we would very quickly find ourselves with no new theoretical results on which to base new practical systems.

The science and technology policy of South Africa's Reconstruction and Development Programme (RDP) had clear guidelines on what scientific research at technikons and universities would be most appropriate for the country. In particular, it stated that government should make such research 'more responsive to the needs of the majority of our people for basic infrastructure, goods and service' (ANC94). Nevertheless, in its section on higher education, it stated that 'the higher education system represents a major resource for national development and contributes to the world-wide advance of knowledge'. Current government policy reaffirms the importance of South Africa playing its part in international and basic research. At the same time, national imperatives *do* mean that there will be increased focus on research relevant to the country, and government funding will reflect this.

17.2 WHAT ARE SOUTH AFRICA'S NEEDS?

The RDP contained five broad programs:
a) meeting basic needs;
b) developing human resources;
c) building the economy;
d) democratising the state and society; and
e) implementing the RDP.

The following list, based on the RDP and the NRF focus areas (NRF01), gives some issues that are extremely relevant and in need of research:

- providing jobs and dealing with unemployment;
- dealing with the land issue;
- providing low-cost, quality housing;
- providing, sanitising and conserving water;
- electrifying the country;
- providing telecommunications;
- developing transport;
- providing health care to all;
- developing social welfare systems;
- providing accessible, quality education;
- rectifying gender and racial imbalances;
- democratising society;
- generating sound industrial policy;
- describing, understanding and conserving our biodiversity resources;
- understanding rural and urban development;
- managing and developing human resources;
- developing information and communication technology; and
- understanding the effects of globalisation on South Africa.

Chapter 18

Case Studies

Our first case study is in the field of chemical engineering, and focuses on water purification (Swa93). It covers the experimental comparison of different filtering methods.

Our second case study is in the field of data communications (Mel89). It addresses a particular problem in communication systems that involve bouncing signals off meteor trails.

For our final case study, we look at an example from medicine involving the health of pregnant women (Qol95). The research looked at the numbers of women in South Africa who have specific diseases during pregnancy.

CASE STUDY 1: A COMPARISON OF FILTRATION METHODS

This case study could also be called 'Building a Better Muck-trap!'

Using common water supplies to provide drinking water requires filtration and purification. Given that one has to deal with a mixture of liquids and solids, filters are often used to separate the two. In particular, microfilters are used to separate the finer (colloidal) particles from the suspension. The research was aimed at comparing two different methods of microfiltration.

The Research Problem

Two common methods of microfiltration are crossflow microfiltration (CFMF) and dead-end mode microfiltration (DEMF). In both cases, the goal is to take the suspension and separate the permeate (liquid) from the solids. The turbidity of the suspension is a measure of how 'thick' it is.

Traditionally, CFMF has been favoured when the main objective is to recover the permeate (from a suspension with low turbidity), and DEMF has been favoured when the main objective is to recover solids (from a suspension with high turbidity). The objective of this project was to establish criteria for the choice between CFMF and DEMF.

Experimentation

The researcher experimentally measured the performance of both CFMF and DEMF for synthetic suspensions over a wide range of input turbidities. Performance criteria included the rate at which permeate is produced and the turbidity of the permeate.

Results and Implications

The researcher found that, for low turbidities, which are typical of raw surface waters such as rivers and streams, the performance of DEMF was similar to CFMF, provided that the DEMF was precoated with a limestone suspension prior to the introduction of the input suspension.

This has significant implications for the treatment of water to make it drinkable. CFMF requires a much larger pumping capacity and consumes much more energy than DEMF does. Therefore DEMF is preferred where energy is scarce (such as in rural communities). It is also possible to use DEMF without any pump at all by using 'natural heads' – such as weirs across rivers – where the falling water provides the necessary pressure.

The Write-up

The study was reported in a masters thesis by A. F. Swart, entitled 'Considerations in the Selection of an Operating Regime for Microfiltration' (Swa93).

CASE STUDY 2: CLASSIFYING METEOR-TRAIL REFLECTIONS

One branch of data communications is that of meteor-burst communication (MBC). Meteors burn up in the upper atmosphere and leave behind trails of ionisation. Electronic engineers have developed a method of using such trails as cheap 'satellites'. They use the trails to reflect radio waves sent up from one point on the earth's surface down to another point up to about 2 000 km away. The fact that billions of these meteors collide with the earth's atmosphere every day makes such communication far more practical than it may sound at first.

The Research Problem

Optimising data communications by MBC is complicated by the fact that trails vary in duration and size, so that signals reflected from different trails have different durations and signal strengths. The problem of determining what types of trails occur naturally is important for a number of reasons. First, it is necessary to know the proportions of the various types of trails if optimal fixed-data rates are to be chosen. Second, if a data rate that can change during the course of the trail is used, then information about the first part of the trail must be used to predict the strength and duration of the next part – which is an impossibility if there is no idea of what different entire trails look like.

The Literature Study

A literature study revealed that previous researchers had attempted to describe trails by looking at the trail reflections. They transmitted a radio signal that was reflected by the trail, and the receiver measured the signal strength over time. Therefore, the classification was done on the basis of time and amplitude. Theoretical work had indicated that trails would be in one of two classes, underdense or overdense, with distinctive shapes (see Figure 11, below: the underdense trail is the smaller of the two curves). However, practical studies had found up to five different classes.

Figure 11: Underdense and overdense trails

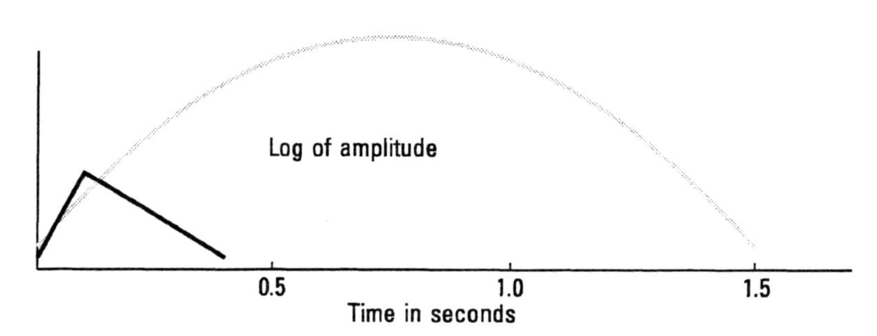

The Researchers

A large team was involved in a cross-disciplinary effort funded by Salbu (Pty) Ltd. The research was based in the Department of Electronic Engineering at the University of Natal, Durban, but members of the Computer Science and Mathematics departments were also involved, as were Salbu's research and development team.

Data Collection

A team set up receiving stations in the small Western Cape town of Arniston and Durban to record meteor trail reflections from links to Pretoria, in order to compare links of different distances. The team eventually recorded essential characteristics (including amplitude samples, background noise and start time) of several millions of reflections and stored them on computer. This data forms the basis of several projects and papers.

The data had to be 'cleaned', as occasional power surges and other sources of noise had corrupted some recordings. Recordings with clearly contradictory data were tagged as 'unreasonable', and the noise was separated out.

Method

The first step was to transform the recordings into a form people could deal with. The team devised a computer program to graphically display time, amplitude and background noise. They then designed a computer expert system to interact with the computer to define various classification rules that distinguished amongst different 'shapes' of trail reflections. These rules were based on 'feature-detection' computer routines (such as fitting lines and parabolas). The experts used an initial base of two rules, one to detect underdense trails, the other a 'don't-know' category. They viewed all trail reflections in each classification separately. Anomalies and sub-families were detected, and the experts fine-tuned existing rules to remove anomalies and introduced new rules to make new categories for the sub-families. They then reclassified all trails according to the new rules, and repeated the process.

Results

The approach described above took several months before the team agreed that no significant sub-families existed in any category, and that there were no outstanding anomalies. The team identified 27 distinct types of meteor-trail reflections, which was a far more detailed classification than anyone had previously achieved.

The team tested the reliability of the results by running the classification system on a control group of trail reflections that had not been used in the classification process, including trails that had been recorded over other MBC links. The discovery that these trail reflections had similar proportions in the various categories, and that there were no visible anomalies, lent strong support to the hypothesis that these 27 categories did constitute a general classification system for meteor-trail reflections.

The Write-up

The team submitted the results of the classification research to the journal *Transactions of the SAIEE* in September 1988, and the article was published in the September 1989 issue. Its title was 'The Classification of Meteor Trail Reflections by a Rule-Based System', and it was authored by S. W. Melville, J. D. Larsen, R. Y. Letschert and W. D. Goddard. The work was subsequently used in further research in both South Africa and the United States.

CASE STUDY 3: THE BENEFITS OF RESCREENING FOR DISEASES DURING PREGNANCY

The Research Problem

A pregnant woman's first visit to a clinic is a major event. She is given a comprehensive medical check-up that includes tests for specific diseases that can affect the mother's health, complicate the pregnancy or affect the health of the unborn child. This process is called **screening**.

For some of the diseases, action can be taken if they are detected in time. Another potential problem is the human immunodeficiency virus (HIV), which eventually causes AIDS. Though HIV/AIDS is at present incurable, it is known that certain drugs may stop the transmission of the virus from the mother to the child (see NRF00). Hence, if doctors detect the presence of the virus, they can take action to protect the unborn child.

However, some of these problems may develop only later in the pregnancy and so will not be detected at the initial screening. For example, there is a window of several months from the time of infection with the HIV virus until the time that it is detectable, or infection may occur after the first visit. So it is best if the mothers are screened again later in the pregnancy. This is known as **rescreening**.

In South Africa, rescreening is not always possible or affordable, and consequently many mothers are not rescreened. The researchers set out to see what the potential benefits of rescreening would be. They were motivated by the knowledge that certain infections are common in South Africa. Specifically, they looked at the incidence of the sexually transmitted infections syphilis and HIV, and compared the results at the initial screening and at birth.

The Researchers

The five researchers were from the Faculty of Medicine at the University of Natal. Three were lecturers there and two were registrars (i.e. physicians studying to be specialists) at the time of the research. The latter included the principal author of the article that resulted from the research, D. C. Qolohle. The research required knowledge of several branches of medicine, so the authors came from the departments of Obstetrics and Gynaecology, Medical Microbiology, and Virology.

Procedure

Having settled on the research problem, the researchers designed the research. They chose a case-study approach. They selected a random sample of mothers coming to be screened and obtained informed consent for serological testing (in which body fluids are analysed for components of the immune system such as antibodies). The team tested the women for syphilis on an individual basis, then told them the results and administered treatment if necessary. They did the test for HIV anonymously, and only the total number of such cases was recorded.

They also collected other information. This included the overall incidence of the infections, a comparison of the infection rate in mothers who came to antenatal tests and those who were seen for the first time when the baby was born, and the incidence of the hepatitis B virus.

Other aspects of the design included the instruments and the data-analysis tools the researchers used, and they also had to choose a serological test to use. Obviously they used the same test on all patients. For the statistics tests, they chose a 5% level of significance.

Results

In the initially screened group of 191 pregnant women, 13 tested positive for the HIV virus at the initial screening and 17 at the final screening. This increase of 4 yields a 95% confidence interval of 0.0–4.4. (The confidence intervals are explicitly given in the text of the journal article.) The researchers claimed that this 2.2% increase indicated strong grounds for re-screening.

For syphilis, the overall infection rate was around 9.3%. Of the 329 women who were screened initially but found to be negative, 9 were found to be positive at delivery, an increase of 2.7%. The researchers obtained a 7.7% prevalence of HIV-positive women (95% confidence interval: 5.1–10.3). This was contrasted with previous studies in the KwaZulu-Natal area, which had found 1.6% in 1990, 2.9% in 1991 and 4.8% in 1992. The data for the study were gathered in 1993. The trend was alarming indeed, and the prevalence has continued to rise (see NRF00).

The Write-up

The title of the article is: 'Serological screening for sexually transmitted infections in pregnancy: is there any value in re-screening for HIV and syphilis at the time of delivery?' The paper starts with a brief abstract comprising a series of short paragraphs under the headings 'Objective', 'Setting', 'Method', 'Results' and 'Conclusion'. Apart from the description of the actual data collected, there is also a discussion of related work both in South Africa and world-wide. Some of the patterns in the data seemed strange to the authors, and they point this out and suggest that further research is needed. The paper concludes with an acknowledgement of the financial support of the Medical Research Council. It was submitted to the journal *Genitourinary Medicine* in late 1994 and appeared in print in early 1995.

Reference List

All66 Allen, R. E., (ed.), 1966. *Greek Philosophy: Thales to Aristotle.* New York: The Free Press.

ANC94 ANC, 1994. *The Reconstruction and Development Programme: A Policy Framework.* Johannesburg: Umanyano Publications.

Arn84 Arnaudet, M. L. and Barrett, M. E., 1984. *Approaches to Academic Reading and Writing.* New Jersey: Prentice-Hall.

App91 Appelgryn, A. E. M., Beyers, E., Mynhardt, J. C., Niewoudt, J. M. and Van den Worm, Y., 1991. *Social Psychology.* Pretoria: UNISA.

Ast85 Astor, G., 1985. *The Last Nazi: The Life and Times of Dr Joseph Mengele.* London: Weidenfeld and Nicholson.

Atw98 Atweh, B., Kemmis, S. and Weeks, P., (eds), 1998. *Action Research in Practice: Partnerships for Social Justice in Education.* New York: Routledge.

AUT94 Universities and Technikons Advisory Council, August 1994. *A Qualification Structure for Universities in South Africa.* Pretoria: AUT.

Bar94 Baron, R. A. and Byrne, D., 1994. *Social Psychology: Understanding Human Interaction* (7th edn). Boston: Allyn and Bacon.

Bar78 Barrass, R., 1978. *Scientists Must Write.* London: Chapman and Hall.

Ber71 Berry, T. E., 1971. *The Most Common Mistakes in English Usage.* New York: McGraw-Hill.

Bes92 Bester, G. and Olivier, A., 1992. *Psychology of Education: Research Methodology.* Pretoria: UNISA.

Ble00 Bless, C. and Higson-Smith, C. 2000. *Fundamentals of Social Research Methods: An African Perspective* (3rd edn) Cape Town: Juta.

Cam90 Campbell, W. G., Ballou, S. V. and Slade, C., 1990. *Form and Style: Theses, Reports, Term Papers* (8th edn). Boston: Houghton Mifflin.

Car92 Carson, R. C. and Butcher, J. N., 1992. *Abnormal Psychology and Modern Life* (9th edn). New York: Harper Collins.

Cas93 Casti, J. L., 1993. *Searching for Certainty: What Scientists can Know about the Future.* London: Abacus.

Chi82 University of Chigago, 1982. *The Chicago Manual of Style* (13th edn). Chicago: University of Chicago Press.

Coc77 Cochran, W. G., 1977. *Sampling Techniques.* New York: Wiley.

Coh80 Cohen, J. M. and Cohen, M. J., 1980. *The Penguin Dictionary of Modern Quotations* (2nd edn). Harmondsworth: Penguin.

Cur90 Curzon, L. B., 1990. *Teaching in Further Education* (4th edn). London: Cassell.

Dav79 Davis, G. B. and Parker, C. A., 1979. *Writing a Doctoral Dissertation: A Systematic Approach.* New York: Barron's Education Series.

Day89 Day, R. A., 1989. *How to Write and Publish a Scientific Paper* (3rd edn). Cambridge: Cambridge University Press.

Far53 Farrington, B., 1953. *Greek Science.* Melbourne: Penguin.

Fle84 Flew, A., 1984. *A Dictionary of Philosophy* (2nd edn). London: Pan.

Fox86 Fox, M. A., 1986. *The Case for Animal Experimentation.* Berkeley: University of California Press.

Fra90 Fraenkel, J. R. and Wilson, N. E., 1990. *How to Design and Evaluate Research in Education* (2nd ed). New York: McGraw-Hill.

Fre90 Freund, J. E., 1990. *Statistics: A First Course* (5th edn). Englewood Cliffs: Prentice-Hall.

Ger88 Gerdes, L. C., 1988. *The Developing Adult* (2nd edn). Durban: Butterworths.

Gre98 Greenwood, D. J. and Levin, M., 1998. *Introduction to Action Research: Social Research for Social Change.* Thousand Oaks: Sage.

Gro95 *Grolier's Multimedia Encyclopedia*, 1995. Novato: Mindscape.

Hic93 Hicks, C. R., 1993. *Fundamentantal Concepts in the Design of Experiments* (4th edn). New York: Holt, Rinehart & Wilson.

Hog93 Hogg, R. V. and Tanis, E. A., 1993. *Probability and Statistical Inference* (4th edn). New York: Macmillan.

Huy87 Huysamen, G. K., 1987. *Psychological Measurement: An Introduction with South African Examples* (2nd edn). Pretoria: Academica.

Jor84 Jordaan, W. J. and Jordaan, J. J., 1984. *Man in Context* (2nd edn). Isando: Lexicon.

Jut94 Juta, 1994. *Juta's Guide for Authors.* Kenwyn: Juta.

Kan46 Kant, I., 1946. *Critique of Pure Reason.* London: Dent.

Kea86 Kearney, R., 1986. *Modern Movements in European Philosophy.* Manchester: Manchester University Press.

Lan89 Langley, G., (ed.), 1989. *Animal Experimentation: The Consensus Changes.* London: Macmillan.

Lee89 Leedy, P. D., 1989. *Practical Research: Planning and Design: A Basic Text for Courses in Research Methodology* (4th edn). New York: Macmillan.

Lou91 Louw, D. A., 1991. *Human Development.* Pretoria: HAUM.

Mau83 Mauch, J. E. and Birch, J. W., 1983. *Guide to the Successful Thesis and Dissertation.* New York: Marcel Dekker.

McH91 McHaney, R., 1991. *Computer Simulation: A Practical Perspective.* London: Academic Press.

Mea88 Mead, R., 1988. *The Design of Experiments: Statistical Principles for Practical Applications.* Cambridge: Cambridge University Press.

Mel89 Melville, S. W., Larsen, J. D., Letschert, R. Y. and Goddard, W. D., 1989. The classification of meteor trail reflections by a rule-based system. *Transactions of the SAIEE* **80** (1), 104–116.

Mel94 Melville, S. W., 1994. *Style Manual for Dissertations and Theses.* Durban: ML Sultan Technikon.

Moo85 Moore, D. S., 1985. *Statistics: Concepts and Controversies.* New York: W. H. Freeman.

Mox97 Moxley, J. M. and Taylor, T., (eds), 1997. *Writing and Publishing for Academic Authors* (2nd edn). Lanham: Rowman and Littlefield.

Mul87 Mulder, J. C., 1987. *Statistical Techniques in Education.* Pretoria: HAUM.

Net82 Neter, J., Wasserman, W. and Whitmore, G. A., 1982. *Applied Statistics* (2nd edn). Boston: Allyn and Bacon.

NRF00 National Research Foundation, 2000. *HIV/Aids Research in South Africa*, Special issue of the *South African Journal of Science* **96**(6), June. Pretoria: National Research Foundation.

NRF01 National Research Foundation, 2001. www.nrf.ac.za/

Par94 Parker, D., 1994. *Tackling Coursework: Assignments, Projects, Reports and Presentations*. London: DP Publications.

Pet59 Peters, J. A. (ed.), 1959. *Classic Papers in Genetics*. Englewood Cliffs: Prentice-Hall.

Qol95 Qolohle, D. C., Hoosen, A. A., Moodley, J., Smith, A. N. and Mlisana, K. P., 1995. Serological screening for sexually transmitted infections in pregnancy: is there any value in re-screening for HIV and syphilis at the time of delivery? *Genitourinary Medicine* **71**, 65–7.

Ror80 Rorty, R., 1980. *Philosophy and the Mirror of Nature*. Oxford: Blackwell.

Rus91 Russell, B., 1991. *History of Western Philosophy*. London: Routledge.

Squ85 Squires, G. L., 1985. *Practical Physics* (3rd edn). Cambridge: Cambridge University Press.

Swa95 Swart, A. F., 1993. *Considerations in the Selection of an Operating Regime for Microfiltration*. Unpublished masters thesis, University of Natal, Durban.

Ter99 Terre Blanche, M. and Durrheim, K., 1999. *Research in Practice: Applied Methods for the Social Sciences*. Cape Town: UCT Press.

Wad90 Wadsworth, H. M., 1990. *Handbook of Statistical Methods for Engineers and Scientists*. New York: McGraw-Hill.

Wei80 Weiner, J. S., 1980. *The Piltdown Forgery*. New York: Dover.

Wel38 Wells, H. G., Huxley, J. and Wells, G. P., 1938. *The Science of Life*. London: Cassell.

Appendix A

Referencing Examples

The following pages contain examples of how to reference an article according to the three methods described in this book. There are many other established referencing methods: if your supervisor wants you to use another method, then do so. Remember that consistency is important, even down to the question of whether you always put a full stop at the end of a reference list entry or whether you always don't. The reference lists for the example article (a contrived and silly one) were chosen to show how to handle some common problems, as follows:

- Feathers and Hair: how to reference a web page;
- Badstat: how to reference a book that is not a first edition;
- Mori: how to reference a journal with a volume number, issue number and page numbers;
- Baxter and Biggs: how to reference a journal not having an issue number;
- Lockjaw *et al.*: how to reference when there are more than two authors;
- Bardon: how to reference an article in a book; how to deal with a direct quote and an editor reference;
- Mhlape: how to reference published conference proceedings; and
- Maharaj: how to reference dissertations.

1. A REFERENCING EXAMPLE: HAPPILY HARVARD

Abstract

This paper provides an example of referencing according to the Harvard system, while saying nothing of any worth about anything else.

Introduction

Results indicating that articles can be entirely lacking in substance (Mori, 1989: 120–4) are potentially significant to professional academics. It is known that much of what is published has exceptionally small audiences (Barker & Biggs, 1980: 198; Maharaj, 1982: 67–79; Lockjaw *et al.*, 1985: 166), with at least one study (Mhlape, 1992: 33–44) indicating that on average journal papers had more authors than readers. The contention now is that it is not worth reading any academic article. This article will investigate this contention on the basis of a study of journal articles.

Method and Results

Bardon (1980: 15) stated that 'the sum is often less than the good parts of its whole'. So all frequently used articles – those with a value of five or greater in the Idiot's Citation Index (Feathers & Hair, 2001) – were not considered for the study. As just four of the 104 987 543 articles were omitted, according to Badstat (1991: 23) this will not affect the statistical significance of results.

A panel of five intelligent people (randomly selected winners of beauty contests) judged the articles. Their detailed findings are given in Appendix X. In summary, their results indicate that at least two of the 104 987 543 articles did in fact contain original, useful information. These results are consistent with the findings of Maharaj (1982).

Conclusion

The fact that some articles were both useful and original provides compelling evidence that articles do contain worthwhile information.

References

Badstat, O. W., 1991. *Silly Statistics for the Seriously Stupid* (2nd edn). New York: Prentice-Hall.

Bardon, A. N., 1980. Alternate aphorisms. In R. S. Naidoo (ed.), *English for the Barnyard*, pp. 10–20. Boston: Wiley.

Barker, X. T. and Biggs, A. T., 1980. The answer to the unasked question. *Journal of Obscure Observations* **9**, 90–104.

Feathers, A. and Hair, D., 2001. *Idiot's Citation Index*. www.silly.billy.

Lockjaw, J. P., Tetan, U. S., Ty-phoi, D., Play, G. and Hepatite, U. S., 1985. Team publishing. *Funding Today* **12** (2), 166.

Maharaj, S. S., 1982. *An Investigation of Investigations*. Unpublished doctoral dissertation, University of Natal, Durban.

Mhlape, M. M., 1992. Who reads it: The myth of reporting. In J. Daniels (ed.) *Proceedings of the Third Southern African Conference on Publication Pressures*, pp. 33–44, Pietermaritzburg: Natal Printing Press.

Mori, I. M., 1989. Subjective subjects. *Journal of Applied Idiosyncracies* **13** (2), 120–4.

2. A REFERENCING EXAMPLE: NEATLY NUMERICAL

Abstract

This paper provides an example of referencing according to the numerical system, while saying nothing of any worth about anything else.

Introduction

Results indicating that articles can be entirely lacking in substance [8] are potentially significant to professional academics. It is known that much of what is published has exceptionally small audiences [3,5,6], with at least one study [7] indicating that on average journal papers had more authors than readers. The contention now is that it is not worth reading any academic article. This article will investigate this contention on the basis of a study of journal articles.

Method and Results

Bardon [2] stated that 'the sum is often less than the good parts of its whole'. So all frequently used articles – those with a value of five or greater in the Idiot's Citation Index [4] – were not considered for the study. As just four of the 104 987 543 articles were omitted, according to Badstat [1] this will not affect the statistical significance of results.

A panel of five intelligent people (randomly selected winners of beauty contests) judged the articles. Their detailed findings are given in Appendix X. In summary, their results indicate that at least two of the 104 987 543 articles did in fact contain original, useful information. These results are consistent with the findings of Maharaj [6].

Conclusion

The fact that some articles were in fact both useful and original provides compelling evidence that articles do contain worthwhile information.

References

[1] Badstat, O. W., 1991. *Silly Statistics for the Seriously Stupid* (2nd edn). New York: Prentice-Hall.

[2] Bardon, A. N., 1980. Alternate aphorisms. In R.S. Naidoo (ed.), *English for the Barnyard*, pp. 10–20. Boston: Wiley.

[3] Barker, X. T. and Biggs, A. T., 1980. The answer to the unasked question. *Journal of Obscure Observations* **9**, 90–104.

[4] Feathers, A. and Hair, D., 2001. *Idiot's Citation Index*. www.silly.billy.

[5] Lockjaw, J. P., Tetan, U. S., Ty-phoi, D., Play, G. and Hepatite, U. S., 1985. Team publishing. *Funding Today* **12** (2), 166.
[6] Maharaj, S. S., 1982. *An Investigation of Investigations*. Unpublished doctoral dissertation, University of Natal, Durban.
[7] Mhlape, M. M., 1992. Who reads it: The myth of reporting. In J. Daniels (ed.) *Proceedings of the Third Southern African Conference on Publication Pressures*, pp. 33–44. Pietermaritzburg: Natal Printing Press.
[8] Mori, I. M., (1989). Subjective subjects. *Journal of Applied Idiosyncracies* **13** (2), 120–4.

3. A REFERENCING EXAMPLE: EFFECTIVELY FTL

Abstract

This paper provides an example of referencing according to the FTL system, while saying nothing of any worth about anything else.

Introduction

Results indicating that articles can be entirely lacking in substance (Mor89) are potentially significant to professional academics. It is known that much of what is published has exceptionally small audiences (Bar80b, Mah82, Loc85), with at least one study (Mhl92) indicating that on average journal papers had more authors than readers. The contention now is that it is not worth reading any academic article. This article will investigate this contention on the basis of a study of journal articles.

Method and Results

Bardon (Bar80a) stated that 'the sum is often less than the good parts of its whole'. So all frequently used articles – those with a value of five or greater in the Idiot's Citation Index (Fea01) – were not considered for the study. As just four of the 104 987 543 articles were omitted, according to Badstat (Bad91) this will not affect the statistical significance of results.

A panel of five intelligent people (randomly selected winners of beauty contests) judged the articles. Their detailed findings are given in Appendix X. In summary, their results indicate that at least two of the 104 987 543 articles did in fact contain original, useful information. These results are consistent with the findings of Maharaj (Mah82).

Conclusion

The fact that some articles were in fact both useful and original provides compelling evidence that articles do contain worthwhile information.

References

[Bad91] Badstat, O. W., 1991. *Silly Statistics for the Seriously Stupid* (2nd edn). New York: Prentice-Hall.

[Bar80a] Bardon, A. N., 1980. Alternate aphorisms. In R. S. Naidoo (ed.), *English for the Barnyard*, pp. 10–20. Boston: Wiley.

[Bar80b] Barker, X. T. and Biggs, A. T., 1980. The answer to the unasked question. *Journal of Obscure Observations* **9**, 90–104.

[Fea01] Feathers, A. and Hair, D., 2001. *Idiot's Citation Index*. www.silly.billy.

[Loc85] Lockjaw, J. P., Tetan, U. S., Ty-phoi, D., Play, G. and Hepatite, U. S., 1985. Team publishing. *Funding Today* **12** (2), 166.

[Mar82] Maharaj, S. S., 1982. *An Investigation of Investigations*. Unpublished doctoral dissertation, University of Natal, Durban.

[Mhl92] Mhlape, M. M., 1992. Who reads it: The myth of reporting. In J. Daniels (ed.), *Proceedings of the Third Southern African Conference on Publication Pressures*, pp. 33–44. Pietermaritzburg: Natal Printing Press.

[Mor89] Mori, I. M., 1989. Subjective subjects. *Journal of Applied Idiosyncracies* **13** (2), 120–4.

Appendix B

Cumulative Normal Distribution

z prop < z

−3.300, 0.000
−3.250, 0.001
−3.200, 0.001
−3.150, 0.001
−3.100, 0.001
−3.050, 0.001
−3.000, 0.001
−2.950, 0.002
−2.900, 0.002
−2.850, 0.002
−2.800, 0.003
−2.750, 0.003
−2.700, 0.003
−2.650, 0.004
−2.600, 0.005
−2.550, 0.005
−2.500, 0.006
−2.450, 0.007
−2.400, 0.008
−2.350, 0.009
−2.300, 0.011
−2.250, 0.012
−2.200, 0.014
−2.150, 0.016
−2.100, 0.018
−2.050, 0.020
−2.000, 0.023
−1.950, 0.026
−1.900, 0.029
−1.850, 0.032
−1.800, 0.036
−1.750, 0.040
−1.700, 0.045
−1.650, 0.049
−1.600, 0.055
−1.550, 0.061
−1.500, 0.067
−1.450, 0.074
−1.400, 0.081
−1.350, 0.089
−1.300, 0.097
−1.250, 0.106
−1.200, 0.115
−1.150, 0.125
−1.100, 0.136
−1.050, 0.147
−1.000, 0.159
−0.950, 0.171
−0.900, 0.184
−0.850, 0.198
−0.800, 0.212
−0.750, 0.227
−0.700, 0.242
−0.650, 0.258
−0.600, 0.274
−0.550, 0.291
−0.500, 0.309
−0.450, 0.326
−0.400, 0.345
−0.350, 0.363
−0.300, 0.382
−0.250, 0.401
−0.200, 0.421
−0.150, 0.440
−0.100, 0.460
−0.050, 0.480
0.000, 0.500
0.050, 0.520
0.100, 0.540
0.150, 0.560
0.200, 0.579
0.250, 0.599
0.300, 0.618
0.350, 0.637
0.400, 0.655
0.450, 0.674
0.500, 0.691
0.550, 0.709
0.600, 0.726
0.650, 0.742
0.700, 0.758
0.750, 0.773
0.800, 0.788
0.850, 0.802
0.900, 0.816
0.950, 0.829
1.000, 0.841
1.050, 0.853
1.100, 0.864
1.150, 0.875
1.200, 0.885
1.250, 0.894
1.300, 0.903
1.350, 0.911
1.400, 0.919
1.450, 0.926
1.500, 0.933
1.550, 0.939
1.600, 0.945
1.650, 0.951
1.700, 0.955
1.750, 0.960
1.800, 0.964
1.850, 0.968
1.900, 0.971
1.950, 0.974
2.000, 0.977
2.050, 0.980
2.100, 0.982
2.150, 0.984
2.200, 0.986
2.250, 0.988
2.300, 0.989
2.350, 0.991
2.400, 0.992
2.450, 0.993
2.500, 0.994
2.550, 0.995
2.600, 0.995
2.650, 0.996
2.700, 0.997
2.750, 0.997
2.800, 0.997
2.850, 0.998
2.900, 0.998
2.950, 0.998
3.000, 0.999
3.050, 0.999
3.100, 0.999
3.150, 0.999
3.200, 0.999
3.250, 0.999
3.300, 1.000

Appendix C

Critical Values of the Normal z-Distribution

one-tailed		two-tailed	
5%	1%	5%	1%
1.64	2.33	1.96	2.58

Appendix D

Critical Values of the *t*-Distribution

df	one-tailed		two-tailed	
	5%	1%	5%	1%
1	6.31	31.82	12.71	63.66
2	2.92	6.96	4.30	9.92
3	2.35	4.54	3.18	5.84
4	2.13	3.75	2.78	4.60
5	2.02	3.36	2.57	4.03
6	1.94	3.14	2.45	3.71
7	1.89	3.00	2.36	3.50
8	1.86	2.90	2.31	3.36
9	1.83	2.82	2.26	3.25
10	1.81	2.76	2.23	3.17
11	1.80	2.72	2.20	3.11
12	1.78	2.68	2.18	3.05
13	1.77	2.65	2.16	3.01
14	1.76	2.62	2.14	2.98
15	1.75	2.60	2.13	2.95
16	1.75	2.58	2.12	2.92
17	1.74	2.57	2.11	2.90
18	1.73	2.55	2.10	2.88
19	1.73	2.54	2.09	2.86
20	1.72	2.53	2.09	2.85
21	1.72	2.52	2.08	2.83
22	1.72	2.51	2.07	2.82
23	1.71	2.50	2.07	2.81
24	1.71	2.49	2.06	2.80
25	1.71	2.49	2.06	2.79
26	1.71	2.48	2.06	2.78
27	1.70	2.47	2.05	2.77
28	1.70	2.47	2.05	2.76
29	1.70	2.46	2.05	2.76
30	1.70	2.46	2.04	2.75

Appendix E

Critical Values of Coefficient of Linear Correlation

$df = n - 2$	one-tailed		two-tailed	
	5%	1%	5%	1%
1	0.988	1.000	0.997	1.000
2	0.900	0.980	0.950	0.990
3	0.805	0.934	0.878	0.959
4	0.729	0.882	0.811	0.917
5	0.669	0.833	0.754	0.875
6	0.621	0.789	0.707	0.834
7	0.582	0.750	0.666	0.798
8	0.549	0.715	0.632	0.765
9	0.521	0.685	0.602	0.735
10	0.497	0.658	0.576	0.708
11	0.476	0.634	0.553	0.684
12	0.458	0.612	0.532	0.661
13	0.441	0.592	0.514	0.641
14	0.426	0.574	0.497	0.623
15	0.412	0.558	0.482	0.606
16	0.400	0.543	0.468	0.590
17	0.389	0.529	0.456	0.575
18	0.378	0.516	0.444	0.561
19	0.369	0.503	0.433	0.549
20	0.360	0.492	0.423	0.537

Appendix F

Critical Values of the Chi-square Distribution

df	5%	1%
1	3.84	6.63
2	5.99	9.21
3	7.81	11.34
4	9.49	13.28
5	11.07	15.09
6	12.59	16.81
7	14.07	18.48
8	15.51	20.09
9	16.92	21.67
10	18.31	23.21
11	19.68	24.72
12	21.03	26.22
13	22.36	27.69
14	23.68	29.14
15	25.00	30.58
16	26.30	32.00
17	27.59	33.41
18	28.87	34.81
19	30.14	36.19
20	31.41	37.57

Critical values for one-tailed hypothesis with 1 degree of freedom:
5% 2.71
1% 5.51

Appendix G

Answers to Selected Exercises

Chapter 5

5. The matched pairs should be 230 & 200, 190 & 150, 140 & 130, 120 & 120, and 110 & 100. The exact groups will depend on which member of each pair is assigned to which group (the two members of a pair will never appear in the same group).

Chapter 8

4 b) $y = 0.09 + 0.42x$ (y = cinemas, x = cities)
c) 21.1
5 c) $y = 11.83e^{0.81x}$ (x = time)

Chapter 9

1. $\frac{1}{36}; \frac{1}{6}; \frac{1}{2}$
2. $\mu = 4.5$ and $\sigma = 2.87$
3. 0.159 (or 15.9%)
4. $n = 11$, $\bar{x} = 10.982$, $s = 2.648$
CI is [10.982 − 1.779,10.982 + 1.779]
5. [43.41 − 0.95,43.41 + 0.95]

Chapter 10

3. Test statistic $t = -2.277$, $df = 10$
a) accept at 95% and reject at 99%
4. Not necessarily
5. Test statistic $z = 10.61$
So accept at 99% that μ not 60.

Chapter 11

2. $r = 0.998$
A linear correlation exists at the 1% level.
4. Test statistic $\chi^2 = 4.33$
5. Test statistic $\chi^2 = 2.044$
6. $r_{12.3} = 0.32$
7. Test statistic $z = -0.48$
8. Test statistic $t = 3.93$

Appendix H

Some Useful Formulas

$$B = \frac{n\sum x_i y_i - (\sum x_i)(\sum y_i)}{n\sum x_i^2 - (\sum x_i)^2} \text{ and } A = \frac{\sum y_i - B\sum x_i}{n}$$ Linear regression

$$s = \sqrt{\frac{\sum x_i^2 - n \times \bar{x}^2}{n-1}}$$ Sample deviation

$$\bar{x} - z \times \frac{s}{\sqrt{n}} < \mu < \bar{x} + z \times \frac{s}{\sqrt{n}}$$

$$\bar{x} - t \times \frac{s}{\sqrt{n}} < \mu < \bar{x} + t \times \frac{s}{\sqrt{n}}$$ Confidence intervals

$$z = \frac{\bar{x} - \mu}{s}\sqrt{n} \quad t = \frac{\bar{x} - \mu}{s}\sqrt{n}$$ Test single mean

$$t = \frac{\bar{x}_d}{s_d}\sqrt{n}$$ Test for difference data

$$r = \frac{n\sum x_i y_i - (\sum x_i)(\sum y_i)}{\sqrt{n\sum x_i^2 - (\sum x_i)^2}\sqrt{n\sum y_i^2 - (\sum y_i)^2}}$$ Linear correlation

$$\chi^2 = \sum \frac{(o_{ij} - e_{ij})^2}{e_{ij}}$$ Contingency table

$$r_{12.3} = \frac{r_{12} - r_{13}r_{23}}{\sqrt{1 - r_{13}^2}\sqrt{1 - r_{23}^2}}$$ Partial correlation

$$z = \frac{\bar{x}_A - \bar{x}_B}{\sqrt{\frac{s_A^2}{n_a} + \frac{s_B^2}{n_B}}}$$ Test of equality of two means

$$t = \frac{\bar{x}_A - \bar{x}_B}{\sqrt{(n_A - 1)s_A^2 + (n_B - 1)s_B^2}} \sqrt{\frac{n_a n_B (n_A + n_B - 2)}{n_A + n_B}}$$

Test of equality of two means

Index